the Organic
reformation

a new hope for the church in the west

Tom Johnston
Mike Chong Perkinson

To all the church reformers and spiritual revolutionaries out there in the Western Church following in the footsteps of Jesus: Go for it.

The Organic Reformation

Praxis

www.praxismedia.org
Published by PraxisMedia, a ministry of
The Praxis Center for Church Development
PO Box 4878 Manchester, NH 03108

Acknowledgements
We would like to thank those who have helped so much with this book: Dr. Eugene Luke, Jodie McCay, Scott Greenlee (cover art) and Carol Brinson (layout).

ISBN: 0-9822727-1-5
Second Printing: 2012

Printed in the United States by Evangel Press

Contents

❀Introduction
a new hope for the church in the west

"See, I have set you this day over nations and over kingdoms, to pluck up and to break down, to destroy and to overthrow, to build and to plant." (Jeremiah 1:10)

There is a time for everything under heaven - seasons come and seasons go (Ecclesiastes 3:1). So it is with the Church. Throughout the centuries, the Church of Jesus Christ has experienced such seasons - times of revival, times of apostasy, times of fruitfulness, times of barrenness, times of harvest and times of harrowing fallow spiritual ground. We are at one of the junctures of those seasons in the Western Church now, a shifting from what was to what is to come. The rapid transit of culture across the American landscape over the past thirty years has left the American church like a once-productive fishing village, which has been stranded - landlocked by a retreating ocean. The shore has moved a hundred miles and the villagers wonder why there are no fish in the desert. They say, "Why, we've always caught fish here before!" The location of the shoreline changed, but the fishermen didn't move with it. But what is truly sad is that the fishermen still expected to catch fish. It is indeed a time of changing seasons in the Western Church. Such seasons mark a beginning and an ending, an uprooting of dead things with an eye to new, green plantings springing forth with new life.

It is in one of these times we now live and minister.

For two and one half centuries the American church has enjoyed unequaled influence in the culture. We were the center-pole of the society, with all roads leading to us. But no longer. We live in a day of declining Christian witness as a percentage of American population (Olsen, *American Church in Crisis*). The church has a favorable rating of only 3% in emerging generations (Kinnaman, *UnChristian*), and the "sin stats" in the church mirror those in the culture at large (Barna, *The Second Coming of the Church*). Our behaviors are not distinct, and consequently, neither is our witness to Christ. We have been locked in a culture war for the past three decades - a war which we have lost. (The previously cited statistics prove it.) Let's face it, the Church in the West is in difficult straights, and there is decline in almost all sections of the nation. That's the bad news. The good news is that while the Church in the West is in serious trouble, the Church of the Scripture is not. The Church has weathered such seasons in the past, and the Church which Jesus said He would build (ref Matthew 16:18) continues to expand and extend His Kingdom on a global scale. Just not in the West.

The pivot point of transition in the seasons has always been borne on the wind of the Spirit - the winds of change filling the sails of men and women who have rediscovered in their generation, by the grace of God, the truth of the New Testament Scriptures - and what those scriptures said about what the Church should be in focus and content. History has labeled these people reformers, revivalists, and revolutionaries - Christians of every era who have had a holy discontent with the status quo of the Church, driven by a righteous passion to see Christ more completely and purely expressed in His Body. They knew there was something more to the Christian experience than what they had encountered. They could feel the Wind compelling them forward, a harbinger of change, and these devoted men and women became the catalyst for a change of seasons in the Church. Such a change is upon us now. The Wind is blowing! Can you feel Him? Are you being moved within? Can you hear the Wind whisper "There's so much more!" If so, read on.

As the Medieval church era came to a close there was developing an ever-increasing skepticism regarding the hierarchy of the church, both in its abuse of power and utilizing the name of Christ for a personal and political agenda. The rise of mysticism along with the impact of nominalism on scholastic theology and the humanism of the Renaissance left people longing for something or someone they could trust. The papacy had been struggling to find vast sums of money in order to continue to cover the expenses of its opulent living. According to Justo L. Gonzalez, this hierarchical decline began immediately after the peak of papal power in Innocent III (12th century). The popes and antipopes sought to secure funding to strengthen their rival claims to be the legitimate successors of St. Peter. On top of this was the influence of the Renaissance which drove the popes to spend as much of the monetary resources of Europe that they could to finance their indulgence of the arts, frequent wars and various personal intrigues.

This is the backdrop to the emergence of the young monk, Martin Luther in the 16th century. The abuse of power by the papacy resulted in anti-papalism and anti-clericalism mindset, particularly in Germany. One factor that caused anti-clericalism was the poor quality of the clergy. In Renaissance Italy, clergy had no training other than watching, helping and trying to imitate their older (not necessarily wiser) colleagues. Clergy were, by and large, illiterate and most had incomes lower than unskilled laborers. On one side, you had the rank and file in the papacy that were trained and of religious aristocracy, while on the other side, clergy were untrained, illiterate and not respected. In rural France during this same period, the lower clergy held the same status as vagabonds and were virtually indistinguishable from other itinerant beggars of the period.

The church at that time was largely oppressive and brought little hope and peace for individuals - at least very little that did not require a work or an indulgence to be purchased. These indulgences enraged Luther as an exploitation of the natural affection of the common people for their dead. Central to this practice of indulgences was the belief in purgatory made popular by Dante in book of the *Divine Comedy*. Purgatory is believed to be that place the dead go to undergo both punishment and purification of remaining sins, before being allowed to enter into heaven.

The popular marketing line that was used to sell these indulgences went something like, "As soon as the coin in the coffer rings, the soul from purgatory springs." The travesty of it all was that the funding raised by these indulgences went to Renaissance Italy to fund the extravagances of the papacy. For Luther hearing the Divine "yes" in Christ was enough for him to realize that one is justified by faith alone, obviating the need for purgatory and indulgences. And so, the young monk spoke out against those that asserted that a dead soul might be freed instantly from purgatory on payment of an appropriate amount to an authorized ecclesiastical tradesman or, should we say, salesman.

Our day is full of successful churches that suggest you invest in the Kingdom and for your investment, God will bring you financial success, healing and a blessed life. We are no longer pawning off indulgences for purgatory, but selling market share in the Kingdom of God for an immediate return for a better life. Much like the anti-papalism of the Reformation, we have an ever-increasing attitude against organized religion with very little trust in those who wield power within these giant ecclesiological enterprises that specialize in living life well in the now on the sacrificial giving of its constituency. On the other end of the pendulum are those pastors and clergy that have sought out a lifestyle that is "anti" everything, rejecting this life for the life to come. As a result, there is very little enjoyment to be had in this life as have an adversarial posture towards the world at large in hopes of preserving their religious way of life without interference from the Dark Lords of the underworld masked as humans outside their fold.

In all reality, the cultural situation of the church today is not only similar in backdrop to the Reformation but also much like the early church of the first three centuries, particularly like the time that Christ entered the world. The state religion of Rome was not providing the peace and salvation people were longing for and so, the Mystery Religions became quite popular, providing people with an alternative to the state religion of Rome for their hope and salvation.

Religion, however, was in the hands of the Roman Senate, and only those gods deemed as such by the senate could be worshiped. As the empire expanded and people from all over the known world moved to Rome, the diversity of religions increased. In response to this ever-increasing religious diversity, Rome instituted a new cult centered in the person of the emperor. Everyone was required to worship the emperor as deity. Deity meant the Roman emperor was to be worshiped as "the giver of good things."

Christianity was birthed and grew within the cultural environment of the Roman state being itself a religion. The way one participated in the state religion was to recognize deity of the emperor. Of course, a true Christian could not do this, resulting in an increasing tension between the Church and Rome. Over time, Christianity would undergo several persecutions, both local and beyond, as the Church's stand on one God brought increasing challenges in the lives of the early Christians.

Like the early church, we have competing religions, a marginalized church, and pagan values. *Our season is ripe for the incarnation of Christ through His people to manifest and bring hope, salvation, justice, mercy and healing to our people and our land.*

Tipping Our Hand - Things We Are Saying And Not Saying

Reform in the purest sense seeks to return to what is primary and foundational. In this way, the Reformation of the 16th century went back to what was primary and foundational with the intent to take the Church forward. Reformation is then the precursor to revolution. In our understanding of the terms *reform* and *revolution*, they speak about a radical departure from one thing to the passionate embrace of another. More simply, it can be said that,

Reform goes back - Revolution goes forward

Before we can move forward in a spiritual revolution we must return (reform back) to the essentials of the New Testament Church. The foundation of the future Church was laid in the past (tradition passed on I Corinthians 15:3-4). The Reformation is needed to strip away all that has been added to the apostolic tradition and allow the truly revolutionary thing that is Christianity to bloom once again in the West in its fullness.

Every spiritual revolution that has its corollary in the Spirit and Scripture has involved a reforming back before there was a revolution forward. Even Jesus came to fulfill the Law ("reform back"), so that the people could move forward with a revolution that involved, first and foremost, the heart.

The Pharisees were all about reform as well. Their primary concern was the reform of Israel. God had abandoned Israel to the Roman yoke because of Israel's unfaithfulness to the heart of God in the Torah. A reform without the heart will be nothing more than a systemic shift back to original principles and foundations that lack the heart that gave birth to them.

In every generation there is a plethora of people who possess good-will, appreciate the problems of culture, and are willing to do anything to help bring lasting change. But like so many, we feel powerless to bring change and don't know where to start. What can one individual or a collection of individuals do anyway? We remind you that it only took 120 fully devoted followers of Christ to turn the then-known world upside down with the Gospel of the Kingdom. In our day and age, it only took 18 men fully devoted to the cause of evil to change our Western world as they boarded airplanes on September 11, 2001. Apparently it doesn't take a lot of people, but it does take those who are fully devoted.

Albert Nolan in his *Jesus Before Christianity* provides some excellent commentary for us.

> *What we are up against is not people but the impersonal forces of a system which has its own momentum and its own dynamics. How often one hears the cry of hopeless resignation, 'You cannot fight the system.' This indeed is the heart of the problem. We have built up an all-inclusive political and economic system based upon certain assumptions and values and now we are beginning to realize that this system is not only counter-productive-it has brought us to the brink of disaster-but is has also become our master. Nobody seems to be able to change it or control it. The most frightening discovery of all is that there is nobody at the helm and that the impersonal machine that we have so carefully designed will drag us along inexorably to our destruction...The system is a monster which devours people for the sake of its profits. (9-10)*

The church struggles with the same as it seeks to find a way out of the matrix (the computer generated reality in the movie, *The Matrix*). Christ has already come and broken the power of the matrix, those impersonal forces driven by the darkness of Hell, so that we, the Church, might be able to stand as one and charge the gates of Hell bringing life, hope and salvation. May the revolution find willing participants who will do just this.

R.E.A.D. Questions

Each chapter in this book will have a series of questions. Using the acronym R.E.A.D., these questions will help you **R**eflect, **E**valuate, **A**djust and **D**o.

Wisdom in the Holy Spirit comes from reflecting on biblical truth. Evaluation allows you to evaluate your current ministry praxis in light of a biblical world-view. This allows you to adjust your life and ministry accordingly (read, repent).

The questions at the end of each chapter are framed within the context of applied theology (theology that seeks to live out what it knows) which encompasses every aspect of our life - our identity, capacity and destiny in Christ. However, we will use an artificial construct of "life and ministry practice" to help you self-evaluate within the broader, prevalent thinking in the Western Church. Prayerfully reflect upon each question and allow the Holy Spirit to nourish your soul and establish a base of wisdom that will allow you to navigate through the tumultuous waters of ecclesiological life.

the Dream
of the kingdom

When God broke into our reality in the person of Jesus Christ, He did so with a dream in His heart - the dream of reunification with His lost children, and a restoration of all things unto Himself (Colossians 1:20). That Re-gathering was to be undertaken by the expression of His kingdom - His royal, sovereign dominion, expressed in the hearts and lives of men and women - His children, and ultimately, over all time-space and the dimension beyond.

Abraham Joshua Heschel says,

> *The world is torn by conflicts, by folly, by hatred. Our task is to cleanse, to ilumine, to repair. Every deed is either a clash or an aid in the effort of redemption. Man is not one with God, not even with his true self. Our task is to bring eternity into time, to clear in the wilderness a way, to make plain the desert a highway for God. 'Happy is the man in whose heart are the highways.' (God in Search of Man 357)*

This was the dream Jesus came proclaiming - the Gospel of the Kingdom, the good news of God's right to rule in the affairs of humankind and the benefits to that humanity of His rule. It was to this dream He called us:

> *Now after John was arrested, Jesus came into Galilee, proclaiming the gospel of God, and saying, "The time is fulfilled, and the kingdom of God is at hand; repent and believe in the gospel." (Mark 1:34-35)*

Jesus spent a lot of time trying to explain to people what God's Kingdom rule was like, and how the dominion would emerge as an *organic process of life-on-life*:

> *And he said, "The kingdom of God is as if a man should scatter seed on the ground. He sleeps and rises night and day, and the seed sprouts and grows; he knows not how. The earth produces by itself, first the blade, then the ear, then the full grain in the ear. But when the grain is ripe, at once he puts in the sickle, because the harvest has come." (Mark 4:26-29)*

Jesus often used organic metaphors to describe the substance and nature of the Kingdom. Some would say this is because he spoke within the context of agrarian society. While this may be true, we think it's more than that. It seems to us that Jesus used these life metaphors because the Kingdom is about *life*. Life gives birth to life. A living God gave birth to a living creation, now dead through sin. The dream of the rebirth and reconciliation of all things to Himself is best expressed by His Son in metaphors of life.

Jesus describes the "seed" as the message of the Kingdom, that when received "automatically" (from the Greek *automaton*) it produces the life of the kingdom in someone. Because of this life-giving aspect, the kingdom and its message has an organic nature to it. Life gives birth to life. It is an ongoing process built into our existence by the One who *is* life (Genesis 1, John 14:6). By organic we simply mean *life-on-life* or *life-to-life* which is a direct correlation to life in the Trinity, where those Kingdom residents share the vital life of Christ with others, seeing His dominion extended one heart at a time. We believe this is still His dream for us today, and this dream is the only hope for the Church in the West.

What does this dream of the Kingdom look like in our day? What is our 21st Century application, living out the life of Christ and fulfilling His Great Commandments and His great commission? We believe it is this organic reformation - the going back - which needs to happen in our day, before we can go forward into spiritual revolution. We must return to a Kingdom-centric way of life lived out 24/7/365, holistically without compartmentalization, which produces ministry naturally as an outcome. This is what we will pursue in detail in the remainder of this book. Here is what His dream could look like, lived out in our lives, our families and our churches today. Dare to dream again with us in the Lord for a minute or two:

What if...

Every individual Christ follower in the West were a fully formed disciple of Jesus, growing in their love for God and others, maturing in the Fruit of the Spirit, capable of sharing His words and doing His work; devoted first to Christ, then to His people, and ultimately to His mission?

Every Christian family took responsibility for their own discipleship, and engaged in simple, loving care and concern for their neighbors?

Every local church could become a fruitful, committed community of disciples who loved God, loved others and made more disciples everywhere they went?

Every pastoral leader knew who they were in Christ, knew what they were called to do for Him, had the skills to pull it off, *AND* the character to maintain their integrity throughout it all?

Every new church that was established was based on the "irreducible core" of Jesus' teachings, focusing on *loving God, loving others* and *making disciples?*

Every denomination or church network could become a move of God, energized by the Holy Spirit, vital in the life of Christ, spreading the Gospel of the Kingdom across the planet?

We believe this is possible - not only that, we believe that it is probable. But it won't happen without change coming to the Church in the West. In fact, the change needed is of such a scale that nothing less than a *revolution* will be necessary.

Something has to change....

The culture is slipping away into the hands of the Enemy. The Church has been self-marginalized and continues to decline in the West - the *only* place on the planet where it is *not* growing. A revolution is needed to overthrow the status quo and bring the Church to a place of new vitality. But this cannot be a revolution of destruction, but one that brings life. It's not about tearing down, but building up - and building with the simple principles of Jesus. "Church as usual" just doesn't work - and a reformation is needed to usher in this new era of spiritual revolution in the Church in the West (more on this distinction between reformation and revolution later).

This "organic reformation" is not about angry pastors and leaders who are disgruntled with the Church, who would want to use the platform of this move of God to execute their own personal agendas, and seek relief from their personal torment and pain. Rather, the reformation is about pastors and leaders who are hungry for more, who realize that what the world calls "success" is not necessarily the same as obedience to God, that making an impression is not the same as having an impact, and that having a crowd is not the same as having disciples of Christ. They realize that transforming a neighborhood, a town, or a city can only take place where individuals and families are transformed, and that the people that comprise the Community of Faith called the Church actually love God and love each other, living out the biblical reality of genuine *koinonia*.

This reformation is an ever-growing movement in the landscape of Western Christianity and is igniting the passion of men and women of faith of various theological persuasions, age groups, and ethnicities to live out and incarnate a transformed Christian faith. This transformed faith seeks nothing less than encountering God authentically and daily, desires to see the total transformation of the self, our families, neighborhoods, and cities, and also strives to see the Church living together as the family of God, a community of God's sons and daughters. These men and women, these spiritual revolutionaries and reformers, are willing to "pay any price, bear any burden, meet any hardship" in pursuit of Jesus and His Kingdom.

The reformation is about *being* the Church, not just *doing* church. It is about living out what matters most in life and settling for nothing less than becoming disciples that have been so captured by the love of God in such a way that captivates the world around them. Still interested? Then read on - *and join us in the Organic Reformation.*

It's your choice....

So, how do we get there? Well, since everything about the Christian life is about incarnation, the Organic Reformation will emerge through the transformation of people - specifically pastors and leaders. The needed change will not happen to the people in the churches until it first happens in the heart of our pastors and leaders.

Make the Dream of the Kingdom a reality in your life and ministry. Join the reformation and become a catalyst for change in the Church in the West. Engage with Jesus and be transformed! The Dream is real. The Organic Reformation has begun. It is happening. The choice is yours.

Reflect

What has God spoken to me through this chapter?

_____

_____

What have I heard the wind of the Spirit saying to me?

_____

_____

Evaluate

Where have I allowed myself to settle in the system (matrix) and not facilitate reform?

_____

_____

Am I experiencing a reformation in my own heart - a revitalization of my love for my Father?

_____

_____

Adjust

What in my heart and thinking, life and ministry practice is God challenging through this chapter?

_____

_____

Do

What will I do to embrace the needed changes?

CHAPTER TWO

_____

_____

_____

The Reformers

Reformers! History is replete with them. All kinds - social, religious, political, in every society, in every age, amongst a diversity of cultures. They are the catalytic agents of change who have seen a different future from the reality that is before them. Dr. Martin Luther King, Jr. had such a vision - even as he helped foment a social revolution within our country, restoring the equity between blacks and whites, we believe that there needs to be a spiritual revolution in the church of the West, leading to a great awakening in the world. For this to occur, there will need to be some catalytic people that are so burdened by the status quo, who see the potential of a vastly different future for their constituency, that they will rise up and work vigorously for the needed change to occur. Martin Luther King, Jr. worked to see change come in the country he loved, the United States of America, for the people he loved, the black community, which continued to suffer the harsh realities of discrimination through interposition and nullification - law being used against law. He was an *intentional reformer* - he saw a vision, which gave him a cause, which defined his mission. King saw a nation rich with equality, in which justice for all people prevailed. The realization of this vision became his cause, his hope shaping his mission.

His vision was embodied most classically in his speech delivered on the steps of the Lincoln Memorial on August 28, 1963. King, departing from his prepared text at the prompting of gospel singer Mahalia Jackson's exhortation, "Tell them about your dream, Martin. Tell them about the dream," on the spot adapted and expanded upon part of the Reverend Archibald Carey, Jr.'s speech to the Republican National Convention in 1952. What is truly amazing is that here he switches from prophetic indictment of current social ills into an equally prophetic dream of the future he saw. What he described is most often viewed in the context of "civil rights," but this young preacher folds in references to Psalm 30:5 and Amos 5:24, painting a picture of what a society impacted by the Kingdom of God would look like. What is the Kingdom issue here? Justice. The word justice or its antonym, injustice, is used eleven times in the speech. He wasn't just talking about humanity. He was painting a picture of the Kingdom of God, and that's what good reformers always do. He had, in his own context, a vision for the Kingdom. Look at his dream:

So I say to you, my friends, that even though we must face the difficulties of today and tomorrow, I still have a dream. It is a dream deeply rooted in the American dream that one day this nation will rise up and live out the true meaning of its creed - we hold these truths as self-evident, that all men are created equal.

I have a dream that one day on the red hills of Georgia, sons of former slaves and sons of former slave-owners will be able to sit down together at the table of brotherhood.

I have a dream that one day, even the state of Mississippi, a state sweltering with the heat of injustice, sweltering with the heat of oppression, will be transformed into an oasis of freedom and justice.

I have a dream that my four little children will one day live in a nation where they will not be judged by the color of their skin but by the content of their character. I have a dream today!

I have a dream that one day, down in Alabama, with its vicious racists, with its governor having his lips dripping with the words of interposition and nullification, that one day right there in Alabama, little black boys and black girls will be able to join hands with little white boys and white girls as sisters and brothers.

I have a dream that one day every valley shall be exalted, every hill and mountain shall be made low, the rough places will be made plain, and the crooked places will be made straight, and the glory of the Lord will be revealed, and all flesh shall see it together.

This is our hope. This is the faith that I go back to the South with.

With this faith we will be able to hew out of the mountain of despair a stone of hope. With this faith we will be able to transform the jangling discords of our nation into a beautiful symphony of brotherhood. With this faith we will be able to work together, to pray together, to struggle together, to go to jail together, to stand up for freedom together, knowing that we will be free one day...

And when we allow freedom to ring, when we let it ring from every village and every hamlet, from every state and every city, we will be able to speed up that day when all of God's children, black men and white men, Jews and Gentiles, Protestants and Catholics, will be able to join hands and sing in the words of the old Negro spiritual, "Free at last, free at last; thank God Almighty, we are free at last." (Martin Luther King, Jr. I Have A Dream 101-106)

Even as he had a dream of racial equality and social opportunity for all people regardless of color, we have a dream of a Church unfettered of its own self-imposed limitations. A Church such as we have described is fruitful, vibrant and empowered by the Holy Spirit, and does not seek to make a difference but *is* the difference within a neighborhood, town, city, culture, state, and the world. Martin Luther King, Jr. was an intentional reformer, and we seek to be intentional reformers as well.

There have been some reformers throughout history that have been *unintentional reformers*. When the monk, Martin Luther nailed his 95 Theses to the door of the castle church in Wittenburg, Germany in October of 1517, he was not intending to catalyze a movement. Rather, he was seeking to dialog about what he felt were key issues within the contemporary Roman church. Indeed, he was seeking to reform, but from within. So, while he was seeking to intentionally bring reform, he did not intend to start what became the Protestant Reformation. At the confluence of many forces in history and European society at the time, Luther nonetheless was swept up by these forces, some say providential-ly so, leading to the formation of Protestantism as a movement. John Calvin, Ulrich Zwingli and others who flowed into the Reformation after Luther did so intentionally. Amazing isn't it, how an unintentional reformer paved the way for those who wanted to press the Reformation intentionally?

Luther saw that the current reality of the Church he was experiencing did not line up with the Kingdom reality of the Church as described in the Scripture, and in pressing the point unintentionally was instrumental in catalyzing a movement. Those who came after him into this reforma-tion also saw this disparity, and moved intentionally within their day to address it. While the Roman church had great power in politics and socie-ty - indeed, it was a temporal kingdom in many respects - they saw it as divergent from the true power of God's Kingdom. They had a vision for more: they had a vision for the Kingdom. Unfortunately, the cultural forces mentioned earlier were also in play - they were men of their times - and what we have inherited in the West 500 years later is still far from a Kingdom-centric Church. Yet, the vision for the Kingdom lives on.

There is still another type of reformer. Some are *unwilling* reformers. Moses, the great Law-Giver of ancient Israel is perhaps the quintessential example of this type - not wanting to go to Pharaoh on Yahweh's behalf (Exodus 3-4), and yet being used by God not only to set His people free, but to reorganize their religious thought, belief and practice. Moses, ex-prince of Egypt, provoked by injustice to the foolishness of murder (an attempt to bring change in his own strength), now a migrant shepherd, a man reticent to be used by God, became the arbitrator of the Covenant - and changed Israel, and human history forever. He had a vision for the

Kingdom as expressed in the Promised Land. Because of his foolishness in striking the rock (Numbers 20:2-13) he was restrained from entering the Land (Numbers 20:12), yet by grace he indeed set foot into that Land (Matthew 17:3). The Church, by its foolishness, has missed entry into the fullness of what it can and should be, and by God's grace we are rediscovering what it is He intends for us. Not to devalue what has gone on before - we value and cherish the Church in all its forms throughout all its history. Yet we can still have a vision for a Church that has a fuller expression of the Kingdom, as we believe this is God's original intention.

Within the Old Testament we see two major crossings: The Red Sea Crossing and the Jordan River Crossing. These crossings illustrate for us where the Church in the West is today.

The Red Sea crossing is what we would call a "Crossing of Desperation." So much of the Church in the West has been in this state of desperation, particularly since the advent of post-modernity.

In this Crossing of Desperation, Israel followed Moses and the promise that God would deliver them. There was initially hope and promise of a future. This hope quickly faded as Israel was led right to the Red Sea. Israel is trapped by the Red Sea in front of them and the Egyptians behind them. God instructs Moses to hold out his staff and so begins the great miracle that brought forth the people of Israel. However, if you read Scripture closely, you will notice that the parting of the sea took all night: "Then Moses stretched out his hand over the sea, and the LORD drove the sea back by a strong east wind all night and made the sea dry land, and the waters were divided" (Exodus 14:21). Can you imagine standing there with your staff held high and the only thing that begins to happen is a massive wind storm? As the winds continue, the sea parts and we see that Israel is being delivered. Life is on the defensive for Israel much as it is for the Church in the West. The Israelites have no options other than trusting God for their deliverance or return to a life of bondage in Egypt. It is interesting that desperation tempts us to return to our bondage or previous life. Fear leads the Israelites to believe that the bondage of Egypt was better than where they are now (Exodus 14:12; John 21:3). Maybe this has something to do with why so many in God's Kingdom live a life of bondage. It is also interesting to note that Israel is being pursued by the enemy and their only hope is deliverance by the mighty hand of God.

Then we have the Jordan River Crossing. Israel followed the "Ark of the Covenant" and the obedient priests into the Jordan River (Joshua 3:3-4). Unlike the Red Sea crossing, the miracle did not take all night but did take several minutes (90 minutes or so). These people, in contrast to those crossing the Red Sea, have already been delivered. In this crossing, Israel is pursuing the enemy, living on the offensive (Matthew 16:18; Isaiah 62:10). We, Like Israel, have a choice to make: to settle for what is good or go after what is promised. Their promise was that of an earthly kingdom, our promise is that of the Kingdom of God. The Church can settle on the near side of the Jordan and not experience the Promised Land or she can pursue the enemy and claim the Promised Land of God's Kingdom revealed in Jesus Christ. We have settled for less than our full inheritance.

If we choose not to enter the Promised Land, and pursue God's original intention for us as the Church, then we will set the stage for desperation. Many pastors are already at this place, with desperation and despair being part of their weekly life in ministry. Let's see how we end up in this place. The stages of desperation are:

Relief
　　(Soul feels the pleasure of control) >
　　　Immediate Results
　　　　(Pathway is now confirmed - it works, therefore it is God) >
　　　　Ache in the Soul/Boredom
　　　　　(Something still missing, success not enough) >
　　　　　Pressure to fix the ache of the soul >
　　　　　Results in increasing stress >
　　　　　Discouragement & Despair
　　　　　　(Ending point for some)>
　　　　　　Demand & Control
　　　　　　(Isaiah 50:10-11, Jeremiah 2:13)

This is what we currently have in the church in the West due to our incomplete obedience and an incomplete Reformation. The Church in the West is standing on the banks of the Jordan River with a choice to pursue: will we settle for what we have or will we pursue the dream of the Kingdom of God, our Promised Land?

Of course, Jesus Christ is the ultimate reformer. Indeed, it can be said that He was and is the ultimate revolutionary. He came to destroy the devil's work (1 John 3:8b) and replace the current fallen order of things *(cosmos)* with one that was from outside (John 18:33-38). He literally came to overthrow the evil empire and restore God's Kingdom rule in the Earth (Mark 1:14-15). But those around Him, both inside His circle of disciples and those outside who saw Him as a threat, misunderstood what kind of reformer/revolutionary He was. He didn't come to destroy, but to give life (John 10:10). He came not to judge, but to save (John 3:16-17) and ultimately, He came to express the Kingdom rule of His Father (Luke 4:14-21). Jesus had (and still has) a vision for the Kingdom, and a vision for the role His Church plays in the expression and realization of that Kingdom rule. We are captivated by His heart, and cannot but join Him in His reformation of His people, and His revolution in the world.

So, what kind of reformer are you? Intentional? Unintentional? Unwilling? Hopefully, you are one after the heart of Jesus, who will fight the good fight of faith, wage the war of hope and abandon all in the pursuit of the Kingdom of God. So, potential reformer, prospective revolutionary, allow us to make our case for the need for a new reformation in the Church in the West, one where the life of Christ flows naturally in His Church and through her to the World, one where the Kingdom of God is a presently experienced and organically expressed reality.

The Manifesto

Every reformation or revolution needs a good manifesto, so we thought we'd start there. Moses had the *Ten Commandments*, England the *Magna Carta*, Luther his *95 Theses*, Calvin his *Institutes*, Westminster its *Catechism* and America its *Declaration of Independence*. OK, so we're not in that league. But allow us to make our point - we believe that there is hope for the Church in the West, but that change needs to come to see that hope realized. We still have a dream: we still have a vision for the

Kingdom of God that He expresses in and through His Church.

We realize there are exceptions to everything we are about to say in this chapter. Our goal is the analysis of trends and situations in the Body of Christ, not criticism. We want to state up front that we are grateful to God and to the faithful men and women of the faith who contend for the real, authentic and lived presence of Jesus. Again, the goal of the organic reformation is to go back to the simple life on life principles taught by Jesus so that the revolution that is the Kingdom can go forward in the West.

This revolution that is on the horizon will involve a reformation of structures and practices, but it is more than that. It is a revolution of heart; a revolution that will ignite the simple passion of loving God and reorienting the followers of Christ to live their lives within the reality of the Kingdom of God as transformed people, living a life based in love that transforms culture. Oswald Chambers spoke profoundly when he said, "Sects produce a passion for souls; the Holy Spirit produces a passion for Christ. The great dominating passion all through the New Testament is for our Lord Jesus Christ" (1455). May the Lord raise up those whose dominating passion is Jesus, to love Him and honor Him with all that we are.

As we write this, we want to avoid the "angry young man" label which some may wish to put on us. We are neither angry nor young, just two guys living with a holy discontent stirred within us by the Spirit of God. While we are not experts, we are also not neophytes - we've lived Church life and been involved in the ministry of the Church for decades. We aren't "anti" anything concerning the Church - we just don't like what it has become in the West. We are not for small churches or large churches; we are for *the Church*, in whatever local form it takes. We are not so much concerned about form, or even doctrine, but *content* - the content of the vital life of Jesus Christ flowing in the lives of Christians everywhere in the West - Christians of all streams, traditions and denominations.

What we share here, we do so hoping to spur the reader on toward love and good deeds - and to foster a reformation that will spawn a spiritual revolution in the Church in the West. So here it is, for the remainder of this chapter, our manifesto.

The Domestication of Christianity

Western Christianity has become rather sanitized and civilized, which has resulted in a sterile faith that focuses more on right and wrong, separation and sin than it does righteous living, inclusion and the Good News of the Gospel. The focus tends to be more on propositional belief statements that lean more towards control than on principles of a lived faith. The Church in the West tends to place its emphasis on personal blessing instead of *being a* blessing for others, the community, and the world. The underlying thought to this seems to be one that believes that if we can control our world and control our God through right practices and behaviors, then we will be blessed and have a comfortable existence.

The Church has become more like a zoo, tame and domesticated, rather than a people who are roaming the wild to impact life. Like the zoo, people come to see the animals of the wild, watch a lion roar, see a tiger, etc. The Church has become a place where we believe that if people come they will be awed and won to Christ. We are trying very hard to be an *attraction*, a *carnival ride*, an *event*, rather than *a people* who embrace a holistic *way of life* founded in Christ. The Church tends to make tame the life that was once in us and then confines its constituency to a cage of respectability and safety instead of releasing people back into the wild where the Church is meant to live untamed, full of love and life in the midst of sin, pain, despair and suffering, incarnating the very presence and love of God.

What is spoken of in our churches is often that of life (the wine) but the focus seems to be more on technique or the wineskin. The wine is about the content of life, specifically the life of Christ within us, as opposed to the ways and means of doing ministry, which is the wineskin. We talk a lot about Christ and His life and yet our focus is not on cultivating that life within us or within our churches but rather on trying to develop better systems, programs and services which we hope will attract people to our church. Our churches are often filled with excellent presentations of life without the substance of it, like a family that invites people to dinner and never serves the meal. Our world is hungry and ripe for an encounter with the living God. In simple language, unless we provide a relational environment for people to encounter God, as we in the Church are encountering Him, then we have done nothing more than creative marketing and have forgotten to provide a quality product. Let us use a metaphor to explain:

The Church is analogous to a family that provides a wonderful meal for their neighborhood. They invite everyone to come for dinner. As people walk in they smell the delightful aroma of a home cooked meal, enjoy the ambiance provided by the followers, the music and the warm greeting by the members of the family. The embrace is so loving that the feeling of belonging and acceptance is near perfect. The anticipation grows for the meal, light snacks are provided to help curb the appetite and build towards the main course. To the surprise of the guests no meal is served. Rather it is described in great detail with PowerPoint presentations and even a movie clip that enriches the picture of the meal for the hearers. The guests leave the house with a great idea of what the meal is but still find that they are hungry. Although the service and hospitality at the house were great, near perfect, they did not meet the great need of hunger within. The guests go elsewhere in search of food to satisfy their hunger. Whether they know it or not, they hunger for Christ and His Kingdom, the presence of which cannot be found in most churches in the West today - and we cannot give away what we do not ourselves have. He is the Bread of Heaven, the Food that satisfies, the Drink that quenches every thirst.

In our churches in the West today we often have the relational dynamics down, the ambiance, the mood-altering worship, technology, the relevant sermons, etc., but we forget to provide the actual meal - the stuff that actually makes us the Church. The atmosphere where a real life God-encounter can take place and people can feast on the Lord to satisfy the deeper spiritual hunger of their souls. People don't go to a sports bar to watch soap operas. Since we are the Church, maybe we should not hold back on what we do, so that people will encounter God as He is. It's one thing for people to come to our churches and leave hungry because we do not provide a meal. It is entirely another for people to come to our churches and experience the meal and find themselves with a choice to eat or not. At least if they leave hungry, they do so because they chose to reject the Lord. We are high on style, and low on substance. That needs to change.

The Church as Vendor and as Circus

Hollywood is no longer the "entertainment capital of the world" - it is now your local church mega-plex or your neighborhood house churches with DVD worship on the 60 inch LCD TV.

The church in the West, bent on attracting people to a location has become a consumer-driven vendor of spiritual goods and services. In short, it has become a circus where the performers are polished and the various acts of the performance timed to the minute. Churches which follow this path often end up **competing for the same market share - Christians in other churches**. (It is still the case that 95% of church growth in the USA is transfer growth.) Whoever has the best product and environment is the one that wins the loyal support of its constituecy. The pressure on the local church is to satisfy its customer base and continue to be a vendor of spiritual goods and services.

But is this really what the church is supposed to do? There is nothing wrong, mind you, with the idea of trying to meet people where they are. We are just questioning the whole concept of "doing church." The New Testament seems to lay a foundation that tells us the Church is a community of disciples who *live out* the message of the Cross. What we don't find in the New Testament is the early Christians trying to "do church." Rather, what we find is a community of disciples who *are* the church. It's organic, it's lived out, and it is not *attended*. You can't "attend church." You *are* the Church.

It seems that we spend so much of our time and energy trying to *do* church that we forget to actually *be* the Church. Maybe that has a lot to do with why the church seems so impotent in its ability to reach our world. We market our message well to those who are already in the faith, but not to those who are outside the fold. Scripture makes it plain that Jesus came "to seek and save what was lost" (Luke 19:10, NIV).

The Church is called to be a community of disciples who not only embrace each other well, but also reach out to the world in a language and style they understand, so that we might live out for them the greatest message on the planet. It's not as important how we "do church" as it is that we *are the church*. This generation is crying out for something real and tangible that can explain the greater mysteries of our existence. People know there is something more; they just don't know where to find it.

What is Christianity: Religion or Revolution?

Jesus came to start a revolution for the redemption of the human heart. Many are Christianized, know the Bible, the principles of holy living, but have not met Christ or do not meet with the Christ daily - instead meeting with the principles and practice, and not the Person. The Way *is* a Person. The Truth *is* a Person. The Life *is* a Person (John 14:6). They have a religion, but don't know the power of it. They have not truly experienced Christ the King and the benefits of His rule. They may know about Him and about the Kingdom, but they know neither experientially.

This revolution, and the reformation within the Church which will facilitate it again in the West, is focused on the powerful person of King Jesus and once again following with biblical devotion. Truly following Christ has always been revolutionary to those who do so, the Kingdom first impacting hearts and lives as an inward reality of "righteousness and peace and joy in the Holy Spirit" (Romans 14:17) and then expressed in a Kingdom community that turns the world upside down (Acts 17:6). This is the movement we need today; this is the Church we need today - the Church rooted in and expressing the Kingdom of God.

The Mission: Reformation to Revolution

As we have said, since everything in the Christian life is about incarnation, this reformation will emerge through the transformation of people - specifically pastors and leaders. We believe that deep within your heart is a passion to see God's Kingdom extended. We can talk with great fervor about the mission and even execute wonderful marketing schemes that boldly declare our message but still lose sight of the one element that is meant to drive the Mission - *love* for God which results in a *love* for people. God is looking for a people whose eyes are wet, who have hearts that are broken and knees that are bent. This incarnational, relational love is what makes this shift in the Church truly *organic*. Again, we define this term as meaning *life which gives birth to new life*, or simply, *life on life*. Machines do not create life, and the Church has become a machine, and not the living, breathing entity known as the Body of Christ. Organic things give birth to organic things - such living things give life to other living things. With the institution of the Church having become mechanized, it has become akin to the Machine world of *The Matrix*.

The mission of this "organic reformation" is to reorient pastors and leaders around what we call the "Irreducible Core" (the "IC") of the Christian life, which will release the spiritual revolution of the Church. We will expand on this in the next chapter, but suffice it to say here that the core is simply living out the Great Commandments (Matthew 22:37-38, Mark 12:28-34, Luke 10:25-28) and the Great Commission (Matthew 28:18-20). Can you image how powerful and yet how simple the Church would be if we just did this? But such power and simplicity will not come without a major shift in both our thinking and our practice. We need another reformation.

Disciples, Not Attendees

The focus of the reformation is on something simple: making disciples. A disciple is someone who is seeking to live the Irreducible Core and is devoted to Christ, devoted to His Church and devoted to His Mission of world evangelization. *The Church in its local expression is a community of disciples, not a gathering of consumers, and has mission as an outflow, or outcome of a way of life (Acts 2:47).*

We need to become a "Fellowship of the Cross." Real community is formed when *koinonia* (Greek for fellowship) is based in mission as in Tolkien's classic, *The Lord of the Rings: Fellowship of the Ring*. We live in a world where *koinonia* or "fellowship" is a commodity that is in high demand but in short supply. No wonder the sitcom, *Friends*, was such a hit for 10 years, as we enjoyed the relationships of six individuals that somehow, in spite of encountering great difficulties, not only maintained their friendships in the series but more amazingly in real life. This friendship was powerfully forged when the actors decided to band together and negotiated their salaries evenly. Whatever one gets paid, they all get paid - they did not like the idea of one being paid more or less than another. The show involved all six actors and all six should get the same paycheck. Now that is a friend, a team, and reflects rather powerfully the biblical definition of koinonia. God help us find this type of koinonia in our churches!

Hollywood powerfully illustrated what a fellowship or true koinonia is in the movie, *The Lord of the Rings: The Fellowship of the Ring.* What Tolkien's world tells us is that fellowship finds it origins in the context of mission. That is, where there is a purpose greater than ourselves, or even the meeting of our own personal needs. Like the nine characters in the movie, who volunteered for the dangerous mission of returning the ring to Mount Doom, we find ourselves in a similar situation in our churches and in our world. There is an evasive evil in our world that seeks to destroy us, and most of those that inhabit earth, including many Christians, who are simply unaware of the danger that looms about us. God has placed it on the hearts of His people to make the journey to Mount Doom, if you will, with the fellowship (that is, of the "Cross") to destroy the evil influence (I John 3:8b). It is a journey that has unenviable odds, enormous obstacles, and armies that outnumber and outclass us at every angle.

It is the battle for our families, our cities, our states, our countries, and even our world. The black gate of Mordor in Tolkien's world stood as an impenetrable obstacle in the quest to destroy the ring in Mount Doom. Scripture makes it clear that the gates of hell cannot prevail against the Church (Matthew 16:18). As in Tolkien's epic, it was a Fellowship that was needed to defeat the forces of darkness, it is only in the "fellowship of the Cross" that we find the full power necessary to defeat the armies of hell. Jesus never said that it would be one church or a single denomination that would be able to resist hell, but the One Church, unified around the Person of Jesus Christ and in the cause of the Mission. It's that Church that hell cannot stop. This is why Satan works so hard to help us focus on our petty differences, find reasons to fight and disagree, gossip, take sides, etc. If he can keep the army quarreling amongst itself it will lose its focus, and fail in its quest. Such was Sauron's tactic in Tolkien's world - to break the bond of fellowship.

The biblical concept of koinonia, the basis of community, cannot take place unless there is a sense of commonality of heart and purpose - a mission that unites us. Koinonia for the Western 21st Century Christian has been reduced to potlucks or coffee and doughnuts. You know, "stay after the service and enjoy the fellowship." True fellowship can only take place where people are willing to share their lives as they share their hearts for something bigger than themselves. This is wonderfully illustrated in Paul's relationship with the church at Philippi. The basis of Paul's thankfulness for the people at Philippi is clearly their active participation with him for the sake of the gospel (Philippians 1:3-5). The word used for partnership is koinonia. Here, it appears that it is referring to an active involvement that would include financial support. Biblical community involves the investment of one's heart in the mission of the Kingdom; which is to love God, love others, and make disciples as you go.

The Church is organic in nature and function, which is not the same as the attraction model or mode that many churches rely upon. This is not to say the Church is not attractive, but rather to clarify that living organisms attract life and give life as a natural process, whereas attraction mode does not bring life or create a living organism. Where life is happening people will be attracted - it is life that is attractive, not the simulation of life.

Mahatma Gandhi once said to some missionaries in India: "You work so hard at it. Just remember that the rose never invites anyone to smell it. If it is fragrant, people will walk across the garden and endure the thorns to smell it." The apostle Peter instructs us to live in such a way that others will inquire of the hope that lies within (I Peter 3:15).

Environment is Everything

It is how we live together in Christ, how we treat one another and relate in His love, that defines us a "church." It is all about the environment the Lord creates in our midst. What the environment of our churches should do is facilitate, enhance, and release the spiritual reality of the new birth in individuals and the culture around us. What the environment of a local church should provide is -

The atmosphere that is most conducive to the creation of life - salvation.

The atmosphere that fosters and allows for the on-going development of life - spiritual growth, as we learn to love God and love others.

The environment by which life can be multiplied - making disciples.

The local church is a spiritual ecosystem where living people learn to live together in their local relational environment. A local church functions as a dynamic and complex whole interacting within the larger framework of the universal Church (the biosphere) - which is the One Church that belongs to Christ. The result is a life of being a blessing, and having unity around the issues that matter in the environment of the Kingdom of God.

The Earth is one biosphere as well as being made up of many ecosystems. The size and scale of an ecosystem can vary widely as it does in the life of the Church. It may be a whole forest as well as a small pond. We even see that different ecosystems are often separated by geographical barriers, like deserts, mountains or oceans, or are isolated otherwise, like lakes or rivers. As these borders are never rigid, ecosystems tend to blend into each other - they are separate and yet, connected. As a result, the whole Earth can be seen as a single biosphere just as the Church is separate and connected, functioning as One Church (biosphere) and yet many churches (ecosystems). The problem is that our churches today function more like individual biospheres rather than part of the ecological whole. We will talk more about this later.

Some Assembly Required

Jesus said that He would build His Church (Matthew 16:18), but it is also clear that He chooses to do that in partnership with us (I Corinthians 3:6-9). *He has reserved for Himself the things which we cannot do, and He has reserved for us those things which He will not do.* So, your participation in the Organic Reformation, and ultimately, in the Revolution that is the Kingdom, is requested. To facilitate the needed change in the Church in the West, we ourselves as leaders in the Church must first be changed. We must throw off our domestication and lay hold of the dangerous, vital life of Christ again. No longer playing it safe, we must risk it all with Jesus once again. Embrace the inner change - and become a change agent in the hands of your God.

This reformation/revolution, as noted earlier, will be one of the heart that will simplify the reality of life and ministry around the Irreducible Core of loving God, loving others as we love ourselves and making disciples as we live life. The process by which this move of God will transpire centers on Jesus, not only for our salvation, healing and freedom, but as the "Way" in which we will do life and ministry. We will share more on this in later chapters.

The Kingdom at Any Cost

What price, the Kingdom? Jesus seems to indicate the Kingdom is only laid hold of through intentional effort (Matthew 11:12), is worth great price (Matthew 13:44-45) and should be the first priority in our lives (Matthew 6:33). Think beyond the cost of salvation, and beyond the salvific event. Think about a way of life that is centered around Christ, His people and His mission of world evangelization. Think beyond "church" as you know it; think how incredible the Kingdom community could be; in its worship, in its life, in its impact upon this dark and fallen world. This is what could be, this is what should be, this is the heart of Jesus for His Church.

The great reformers of the past, both inside and outside of the Church, have realized the great personal costs associated with seeing such a vision realized. Are you willing to count the cost (Luke 14:28-30) for the Church in the West? Yes, you the prospective reformer, the potential spiritual revolutionary. Who else is going to do it? The Father has no "Plan B" - the Church (the people, not the institutions) - you and I and others in the Body are all He's has to work with. I know it is a scary thought - but it's His choice to work incarnationally through His Body. So we must embrace His work of reformation, both in us and through us. We must work the works of our Father *in* His Church so He can work His works *through* His Church. Otherwise the hoped for, prayed for awakening in the Western world will never come. Restoration of His Bride must come, not in the institutions, not in the machine of ministry, but in the vibrant, rich organic life of Christ expressed in His people, His Kingdom community. To this end we must, as John F. Kennedy put it, "pay any price, bear any burden, meet any hardship," but not just for an earthly kingdom or nation, but for an eternal Kingdom, for the person of Christ, to see His people restored, to see His Kingdom come. This is our manifesto; this is our hope for the Church in the West, an *organic reformation* that will again release the revolutionary, life-giving power of the Kingdom of God.

Reflect

What has God spoken to me through this chapter?

_____

_____

Where do I fit in this reformation?

_____

_____

Evaluate

Where have I embraced a domesticated Christianity?

_____

_____

Am I more of a Ringmaster at the Circus, or a performer, or animal trainer - or am I a leader in the Body of Christ?

_____

Adjust

What in my heart and thinking, life and ministry practice is God challenging through this chapter?

_____

_____

_____

Do

What will I do to embrace the needed changes?

_____

_____

_____

the **Heart**
of the kingdom

Back to the Core

Everything in Scripture is important - and everything in Scripture points to Jesus Christ. The reality of the Messianic Kingdom revolves around the person of the King. In order to have a Kingdom, we must have a King - and we do: His name is Jesus. An interesting thing to us is that people in the Church most often fight about the nature of Scripture, rather than simply obeying what it teaches us. As Mark Twain said, "most people are bothered by those passages of Scripture they do not understand, but the passages that bother me are those I do understand." The call to the Kingdom is a call to obey our King, Jesus.

What is essential is that we become obedient to the Scripture. A Holy Scripture is best validated by holy lives that have the fullness of the Kingdom reality within, expressed in love. Jesus himself said, "You search the Scriptures because you think that in them you have eternal life; and it is they that bear witness about me, yet you refuse to come to me that you may have life" (John 5:39-40). True belief in the canon of Scripture can only be displayed by a life lived out in obedience to the King. It is more than a belief in propositional statements about Scripture and what the Scripture says. Rather it is a life that embraces the dominion of God at a personal level. It is the life lived unto to God.

It is an organic reality. It is a way of life that moves beyond mental assent to a series of doctrinal statements and embraces the One the doctrines speak about and the life He now lives in us.

This has been radically illustrated throughout the history of the Church and particularly in the Barmen Declaration of 1934 amongst the Lutheran, Reformed, and United Churches as a response to Hitler's National Church. The individuals that participated were part of the Confessing Church, and they wanted to make clear their confession was to be backed by their very lives. The propositions were not only confessed but backed with lives that chose to live in obedience to the Person the propositions were addressing - Christ.

Our actions verify the true nature of the treasure that is in our hearts. Jesus said that "where your treasure is, there your heart will be also" (Matthew 6:21). Our hearts must be firmly established in His Kingdom, and His Kingdom in our hearts. It is only then that our lives can truly be lived unto God, only then when the Kingdom is a lived, organic reality. While many who claim the name of Christ in the West are positionally within the Kingdom through their faith - they are there salvifically - yet they walk daily under the dominion of darkness because their minds are un-renewed. To some degree, they themselves are not responsible for their current state as they have been spiritually birthed into a form of Christianity with defective DNA. They have inherited spiritual birth defects as it were, which have allowed or caused them to be in their current dilemma. Indeed, they have also been given permission to remain in that dilemma by both the degenerate church culture and the leaders thereof. Yet we look at Romans 12:1-2 and we see that the true worship of a Christian is the organic reality of a life lived out, with that life being lived in pursuit of knowing and doing God's will; in other words, living in the Kingdom dominion of our loving Father.

I appeal to you therefore, brothers, by the mercies of God, to present your bodies as a living sacrifice, holy and acceptable to God, which is your spiritual worship. Do not be conformed to this world, but be transformed by the renewal of your mind, that by testing you may discern what is the will of God, what is good and acceptable and perfect.

What this passage in Romans tells us is that God's will is ultimately knowable - it is not meant to be an unattainable mystery. This passage indicates we can figure out His will ("by testing you may discern") when we do not conform to the fallen order, but are inwardly transformed. We can feel our way towards His will, and find it (Acts 17:27). This transformation is the presence of the Kingdom within us, and when we live our everyday lives - with our families, at our jobs, at school, with our friends, in our relationships, with our finances - we are *actively worshipping* Him. This is the whole life lived unto God that Jesus came to lead us into. He did not come to give us an updated set of doctrines or propositional truths, He came not only to be a sacrifice so that we might have life with the Father, but also to *show us how to live.*

Where the first Reformation was about breaking the authority of cultural and political traditions within the Church and returning to the authority of Scripture, the Organic Reformation liberates us from the cultural and political baggage that has encumbered the church over the past 500 years. We seek to cast off the same encrustation of human tradition and practice, returning us to the simple way of life Jesus taught us. Here we are not speaking of any form of church structure, tradition or polity in particular. We do not feel the New Testament actually prescribes any methodology whatsoever. In this way, the New Testament is formless when it comes to church structure or polity. Any form may be valid based on whether or not it perpetuates the Kingdom life. We are not advocating the rejection of form - the wine does need a wineskin. Nor do we reject all institutional aspects of the Church, as there are places where the Kingdom touches culture and is best served through organizational interfaces with that culture. While the container can be a problem, for the most part we need to focus on the content - making sure that the vital life of Christ is active and flowing in our lives and our church communities.

Our goal, then, is the Kingdom life lived out, and because His will is knowable, it is doable. But first we must strip away all that impedes us, all the cultural and political church trappings that have been wrapped around the teaching of Jesus. We must return to the core of our faith.

The Power of the Core

Jesus defined for us, by His life and words, what life in the Kingdom looks like. His words bring us *illumination* as to the nature of the Kingdom, His works bring *illustration* of His Kingdom's dominion. The Gospel of the Kingdom was and is fully preached and lived out in both His words and His works (we will develop this further in following chapters). Again, it is a lived, organic reality which demonstrates the presence of His Kingdom in our lives. When Jesus came, He came to bring us into the Kingdom, and give us a way of life. From what He gave us in the New Testament, we have extrapolated a *religion* that can be compartmentalized, as opposed to a *way of life* which must be embraced in its totality. If we return to simply what He taught us, we can disencumber ourselves, and His Church as a whole.

Everything He taught us can be summarized into three things that we call the *"Irreducible Core"* of the Christian faith, namely:

> *Love God*
> *Love others (as you love yourself)*
> *As you go, make disciples*

This "Irreducible Core" (or IC) comes from two passages of Scripture, commonly referred to as the Great Commandments (Matthew 22:34-40) and the Great Commission (Matthew 28:18-20, which we shall discuss later in the chapter):

> *But when the Pharisees heard that he had silenced the Sadducees, they gathered together. And one of them, a lawyer, asked him a question to test him. "Teacher, which is the great commandment in the Law?" And he said to him, "You shall love the Lord your God with all your heart and with all your soul and with all your mind. This is the great and first commandment. And a second is like it: You shall love your neighbor as yourself. On these two commandments depend all the Law and the Prophets."*

Jesus said these two Commandments (one from the Shema in Deuteronomy 6:5 and the other from Leviticus 19:18) were the summation of the Jewish Scripture - otherwise known in Jesus' day as "the Law & the Prophets" being common shorthand for the "Law, the Prophets and the Writings," (and what we now call the Old Testament.) One of the key words here is "depend" (as translated in the ESV, RSV & NASB; "hangs" in the NIV and NKJV, and "based on" in the NLT). Everything in the Torah & Talmud, the totality of Jewish Scripture depends on, and has expression in these two things. In using the phrase "the second is *like it*" (laid along side, parallel, equal to) Jesus was indicating that love for others was as important as love for God, indeed that the two things were inseparable. To love God, you must also love and value your neighbor as you do your own soul. The Master Rabbi Himself is telling us that to live in love we must not only love God, but love His image - humankind - as well. Another rabbi offered a similar statement as he said, "For the whole law is fulfilled in one word: "You shall love your neighbor as yourself" (Galatians 5:14).

It is important to note here that Jesus is speaking to an expert in the law. Viewed positively, that meant someone that sought to observe the Ten Commands and the 613 commandments of the Torah because of love for God. Viewed in the negative, the reference is to an expert rule-keeper. This guy's job was to know the rules and teach people how to keep them. He was asking Jesus which of the rules was the most important. Jesus flips the dialog on him, moving away from the rules to talking about *relationships*. He is trying to point out to this Pharisee the original intention of the "rules," or commandments was how to have *right relationships* - as defined by God Himself - with God and with others. Indeed, even the Ten Commandments are given to this end - the first four being about having a proper relationship with God and the second six about having proper relationship with others (Exodus 20:1-17). Set in the tone of negative, prohibitive warnings, they are positively summarized here in this passage as He quotes from the Law itself (Deuteronomy and Leviticus being part of the Law of Moses). He quotes the Law to this Law expert, telling him in a parabolic, rabbinical way - "you're missing the point, you're not getting it. It's really about a loving relationship with God that flows into loving relationships with others." Maybe the Great Commandments would be better described as the Two Great Relationships. Let's look at these two love relationship - with God and others - in some more detail.

We love God because He first loved us (1 John 4:19). If loving God is the first commandment for us as His disciples, then we exist to be loved by Him with everything He is and to love Him in response with everything we are. Our whole life becomes a singular act of worship (Romans 12:1-2 again). Knowing and loving Him becomes our first priority, our individual and collective first response to His love. We should each seek first His Kingdom and His righteousness (Matthew 6:33). Our love for Him, our response to His love for us, should take real form in our lives, as our choices and priorities, which are individually and collectively set around the Kingdom. All this proceeds not only out of a sense of duty, or even human emotion and gratitude, but out of divine love that transcends the self, even calling for Christ-like self-sacrifice. This focus determines individual life-choices, now made with a Christ-centric and Kingdom-centric view of reality.

As a disciple, our personal identity as sons and daughters of God is found in this relationship (1John 3:1a). As individual Christians become more aware of who He is, they can realize who they are in Him. We have written at great length on this subject in our book *A New Testament Trilogy* (100-104) so we will not go into it here in any great depth. The key point to mention is that we achieve self-awareness through God-awareness. As we grow in our understanding of the exchanged life, we grow in the loving definition crafted for each of us by our Father. God's love uniquely defines each of us as His child, and as we grow in the knowledge of Him and as we experience His love, we come to understand our own value as persons. If we do not know Him intimately, and have not experienced His love for us, we are perpetually caught in a quest to self-define, (or in the words of our generation, to "find ourselves.") Through Him, we can have a healthy, proper appreciation of the self, based in our understanding of who we are in Christ.

The key to developing this relationship with God, and coming to understand who we are in Him, *is the cultivation of spiritual disciplines*, first personally, then within our marriage and family, and finally, within our local churches. It is amazing to us that amongst the thousands of pastors we regularly encounter each year we find few who are actually engaged in spiritual disciplines as couples or families. The pastor and his/her spouse may have individual practice of these disciplines, but rarely is there study of the Scripture together, shared spiritual reading or even prayer times together. For children, if there is discipleship going on, it is usually handled by the mother, with the father becoming decreasingly involved as the children age. We will discuss this in more depth later, but we think this is a major issue in the Church, and significantly more so if our leaders aren't doing it. We like to say "If it doesn't work at home, you don't get to export it!" and "You can't give away what you don't already have" (See 1 Timothy 3:1-7). How can spiritual leaders lead others into the embrace of Divine Love if they are not cultivating that embrace for themselves? How can we expect to live those lives of love and devotion, those acts of worship, without such communion? If Jesus said this is the first priority for our lives, we cannot but work on cultivating our relationship with our heavenly Father. This is the first component of the IC.

As we establish ourselves in His love, and know and value ourselves through knowing His love, we can then, as a matter of natural outflow, love others around us. Such loving is now supernaturally natural, and organic expression of His life lived in us. As Paul said, it is now no longer we who live, but Christ who lives within us (Galatians 2:20). It is no longer we who love with our selfish, agenda-driven affection, but Christ who loves through us. I don't love just those who are "lovely" to me, but the unlovely as well - all in the strength of His heart. Having experienced His love, and continually living and growing in the fresh awareness of His love (Ephesians 3:14-19), we *must* love others. We are compelled to by His love, His very nature at work in us has as an outcome of that work - love for others (1 John 4:16). If we do not have His love flowing through us to others, there is something amiss with our soul (1 John 4:20-21). Either we have never truly been impacted by His love, or some significant area of brokenness exists within us which keeps us from both knowing and expressing the love of God.

Maybe this is part of the problem in our churches as we seek to motivate our people to share their faith (evangelize). We come up with all kinds of creative campaigns to get people to profess their faith. Let us suggest that if you have to teach evangelism to your church then it is already too late. You have a heart problem in your church - a love loss. For example, when a couple begins to court and fall in love, there is an immense and passionate desire to be together. You do not have to question if the couple desires to be together. Their actions and words verify that in abundance. Where there is a lack of love people are not aware of the "other". When our hearts are moved by the love of God, we find our hearts loving what He loves and weeping over what He weeps over. No one has to tell the loving couple to spend time together. If anything, we might tell them they are spending too much time together. Love awakens us to the "other" and moves us to bring life and share life with them. Is not that the heart of evangelism - love that motivates and drives our hearts for the "other" to share life and love in word and deed so that they might come to know this most amazing God.

The loss of love becomes the foundation for a life of legalism and self-focus, a preoccupation with one's own spiritual state at the expense and judgment of the "other." This is most clearly explicated in the Pharisee, in Luke 10:29, who seeks to justify himself by pulling it back to the rules: he asks for detailed clarification on who exactly his neighbor is. From Jesus' response we get the Parable of the Good Samaritan. Through this story, Jesus uses a stranger, and a Samaritan no less, to indicate that the *proximity* of relationship is not the issue, love is. In the parable, love demands that the relationship is initiated to care for the wounded man. Those closest culturally, and whom may seem to be the most spiritual - the priest and the Levite - failed to attend to their own fellow religionist and countryman. The Samaritan, more distant culturally (considered to be a mongrel by the Jews) and religiously (thought of as heretical), is here the "neighbor," the one close at hand - at least in the sense of God's heart. How often we use spiritual rationalization to not love, to not care, to not express Christ to those who are not like us, or who would seemingly inconvenience us with their need!

But God's love is calling us back to His heart of love for others. Jesus said such love would be the hallmark of our discipleship:

A new commandment I give to you, that you love one another: just as I have loved you, you also are to love one another. By this all people will know that you are my disciples, if you have love for one another."
(John 13:34-35)

The Apostle John tells us that such love needs to be demonstrated - moving beyond the realm of emotion into that of action - life lived out (1 John 3:16-18). James gives a similar admonition (James 1:27, 2:8; 14-17), as the rabbi of their day would have equated "righteousness" with care for the poor. God's love is meant to be demonstrated relationally in the meeting of the needs of others. This is what the incarnation of Christ, the embodiment of His love, is all about (Romans 5:6-8). We see this lived out in the life of the early Christian community, where resources were shared so that all needs could be met (Acts 2:44-45). What would it be like for the Church to live in such loving community? If knowing and loving God is our first priority, then loving and serving others becomes our second priority. Such love for others is the second component of the IC.

This love for God and others flows into yet another kind of relational dynamic, the making of disciples for Jesus. Let's now take a look at the Great Commission, the third component of the IC:

And Jesus came and said to them, "All authority in heaven and on earth has been given to me. Go therefore and make disciples of all nations, baptizing them in the name of the Father and of the Son and of the Holy Spirit, teaching them to observe all that I have commanded you. And behold, I am with you always, to the end of the age." (Matthew 28:18-19)

No other verse in the New Testament has fueled more missional endeavors than this one, and yet it has been greatly misunderstood. Jesus' command to continue the process of disciple-making - making them now the rabbis - was meant to be a continual life-on-life process of developing His followers. They were not just to teach them what is commanded, but how to do what was commanded. It wasn't just about knowing the propositional truths He taught, but how to live in relationship with the Truth in everyday life (John 14:6). They were to continue the incarnational, relational life-pattern teaching of the master Rabbi, Jesus, spreading His rabbinical yoke to the world. They were to baptize or immerse them into the One ("name of" is singular in Greek) and teaching them how to live the way of the One. The Greek literally translated reads, "Going, therefore make disciples." In English we have historically placed the imperative on "go," but the imperative in the Greek is on "making disciples." The "how" is in the baptizing/immersing in the One and teaching them to keep the way of the One. (Matthew is connecting back to the Shema and highlighting Jesus as the incarnation of the One True God.) Christ is saying to them, "Everything I have shown you and taught you, now go and do."

Matthew's Jewish emphasis, which bridges the Old and New in Jesus, also reveals the Jewish nature of proselyte baptism which allowed the non-Jew to become a Jew and be included in the Jewish way of life and community. This is precisely how Jesus utilizes the word, telling us to baptize, or to bring people into, the One and the way of life in the One - the Kingdom community. Just as John the Baptist had a baptism of repentance that brought the Jew into the Messianic community awaiting the advent of the Messiah, the baptism that Jesus now commands is into the Messianic community that now looks forward to His second coming. It is a community that lives out the Kingdom way of life in relating to God and others. The "as you go" element is what points us not to action or activities, or even events, but rather *to a way of life lived out* 24/7/365, which produces as its outcome more disciples. Again, we see this incarnated in the early Church in Acts 2:47, *"praising God and having favor with all the people. And the Lord added to their number day by day those who were being saved."* Matthew, in both the Great Commandments and the Great Commission, is tying the person of Christ and his "as you go" commission to the disciple back to the Shema in Deuteronomy 6:4-9:

> *Hear, O Israel: The LORD our God, the LORD is one. You shall love the LORD your God with all your heart and with all your soul and with all your might. And these words that I command you today shall be on your heart. You shall teach them diligently to your children, and shall talk of them when you sit in your house, and when you walk by the way, and when you lie down, and when you rise. You shall bind them as a sign on your hand, and they shall be as frontlets between your eyes. You shall write them on the doorposts of your house and on your gates.*

Christ is calling them to, as well as empowering and releasing them, to a lifestyle of disciple-making which is to happen everywhere, all the time, along the way, as part of everyday life. Indeed, they are to go forth with intentionality of making these disciples, but it is to be approached holistically, and not from a compartmentalized framework. In Deuteronomy 6:7 the pervasive "as you go" through life teaching is given as a means of generational transmission. He gave them, and us, the stewardship of the Gospel message, the *euangélion* of the Kingdom, which was to be passed on through the whole life, impacting the whole life, done in sharing His words and in doing His works, living a life wholly consumed in God. In effect, the Irreducible Core becomes a "New Testament Shema," or "Shema 2.0." The goal of the disciple-making New Testament rabbi is then to, through their whole life:

> *Help people encounter and know God and His love for them, and how to love Him through every aspect of their life.*

> *Show people how to live in such a way that the love of God flows out of them as love for others embodied in serving and caring.*

> *Empower these people to themselves be the rabbi, and make more disciples of Jesus Christ.*

This new "Shema" says that the One God has loved us in the person of His son, and that we should reciprocate that love to Him and all those who bear His image, bringing more and more of His lost children safely home to Him again. This is what the Kingdom community is about, and this is what the Church in the West must *again* embrace if it wishes to bear a powerful witness to a powerful Christ. As we have seen, this cannot be accomplished institutionally. There is no program or strategy that can pull us out of the place where we are. We must return to the power of life lived in the IC. As mentioned earlier, this element of individual and family discipleship is key to the Organic Reformation. The faith is transmitted organically, life-on-life, not mechanically through institutions. Father and mothers need to be developed themselves as disciples, to be the "high priests" of their home, crafting a way of life for their families in which to follow Christ. *Every home, as it were, must become a church.* Not in the sense of just a house church format or a bunch of disassociated, isolated Christians. Don't think form, think *function* - the Church, His *ekklesia*, the Kingdom community, which worships God through its lifestyle, and shares Christ with those around it in both words and works - this is the kind of church we propose, the living, breathing Body of Christ, whose presence can be found in every home, every apartment, every condo and every tenement. Only then will we see change come in the church, only then will the Organic Reformation have its fullest effect (but that is another book in and of itself!)

This mission - the calling to make disciples - is driven by compassion. It *must* flow from God's heart to ours; His love in our hearts overflowing into the harvest. The Great Compassion is mission-driven by divine love, not duty, guilt or agenda. What we weep over tells us where our heart is and what we are most compassionate about. Do we weep over the weekly attendance of church services, the low offering, or do we weep of the lost-ness and brokenness of our cities? Jesus wept over Jerusalem (Luke 19:412), and had compassion on the crowds.

And Jesus went throughout all the cities and villages, teaching in their synagogues and proclaiming the gospel of the kingdom and healing every disease and every affliction. When he saw the crowds, he had compassion for them, because they were harassed and helpless, like sheep without a shepherd. Then he said to his disciples, "The harvest is plentiful, but the laborers are few; therefore pray earnestly to the Lord of the harvest to send out laborers into his harvest." (Matthew 9:35-38)

It was love that moved Jesus' heart, love that caused Him to tell His disciples to plead with the Father to compel laborers into the harvest field. And so it should be with us. We should see and engage the harvest of souls before us out of a heart filled with His love. It should be the outflow of our relationship with Him, not just a sense of duty or even one of mission, but because love demands it. Individuals and church communities so motivated by God's heart, they become catalytic change-agents in the Kingdom economy, birthing new moves of God. Such organic movements flourish when Jesus' passion for both the Father and lost people collide inside the heart of a person or persons.

These movements are comprised of the passionate disciples and those they impact - the new converts. As a result, these movements almost always incarnate through the establishment of new kingdom communities of all kinds of shapes, styles and expressions. Such movements are facilitated by harnessing and nurturing such life-flow in the Kingdom. This then allows leadership to add intentionality by "stewarding the grace" (Ephesians 3:2), seeing Jesus build - and rebuild - His Church, just as He promised in Matthew 16:18. (We will discuss organic movements in a later chapter.) This is our hope for the Organic Reformation: that the power of His love will spark again in His people, even as it did in His early disciples, and like them, we will be swept up into a world-changing move of His Spirit which will transform the West. But first we must return to the power and simplicity of the Core.

Rebuilding the DNA of the Church

There is hope for the Church in the West, but significant rebuilding around the Irreducible Core must take place for this hope to be realized. As mentioned earlier, the Church in the West has inherited spiritual DNA which is defective, which has led to its impact on the entirety of its life and mission. There is currently significant dialog about the "missional" aspect of the Church, all for good reason. The fruit of the Church in the West is rather thin and dry, both in its life and its impact on people and culture. The answer may be simpler than it may seem. Let us use a personal example.

Tom was born with a genetic disease called Cystic Fibrosis (CF). While it has many complications and affects, it tends to be terminal for most who have this condition, usually dying by age 35. Right now, Tom is pushing 50, and we are thankful to God for that! However, one of the aspects of the disease is that 97% of males with CF are born infertile. Consequently, Tom & his wife Cathy do not have any natural children. A mutation in a single gene - the Cystic Fibrosis Transmembrane Regulator (CFTR) gene, known as the Delta F508 mutation - causes CF and the resultant infertility. The CF gene occurs on the long arm of Human Chromosome 7 (we have 23 chromosomes), from base pair 116,907,252 to base pair 117,095,950 on that chromosome, and is caused by loss of the amino acid phenylalanine at position 508. Now that you know way more than you ever wanted to know about CF, you must be wondering why we told you all that. We shared this to simply illustrate a point: *the absence of a small piece of genetic material can cause a big problem.* A missing amino acid at 508 means Tom and his wife Cathy can't have kids - they are not able to reproduce. This very, very small genetic flaw causes a host of health problems, including infertility. The Body of Christ in the West has the same problem - it is unhealthy through flawed spiritual DNA - and it can't reproduce! We have, as it were, a spiritual birth defect. To address this, we need some spiritual "gene therapy," by grafting in healthy DNA to replace what is flawed or missing.

DNA could be thought of as the "Irreducible Core" of human biology. It is what is at the core of every person, and will define what that person will look like and be when they are fully matured. We would contend for a three-stranded DNA for the Church, the Body of Christ: loving God, loving others, and as we go through life, making disciples. The Great Commandments and the Great Commission are the ultimate summation of everything Jesus wants to form in us and to do through us. He wants us all to know and experience the Father's love. He wants us all to love each other as a testimony of this love, and He wants us to love those not yet reintroduced to their Father to such a degree that we would commit our entire lives to that ministry of reconciliation (2 Corinthians 5:17-20). It is this DNA which must be infused into the Body of Christ, bringing with it both health and reproduction. In science, when such an infusion of DNA takes place, it is called "transformation." Amazing, isn't it? This is exactly what we seek for the Church, and is the heart of the Organic Reformation.

Loving God, loving others and making disciples is a way of life. We think you can do more than this and be a Christian. However, we do not think you can do less than this and be a disciple of Jesus Christ. It is the simplicity of the IC that the Church in the West must return to if it wants to see the richness of Christ expressed both in its life and its mission. There is power in such simplicity, and a powerful life can be lived and powerful ministry done, all based on the DNA of the core of Jesus' teaching.

Reflect

How has the IC challenged my thinking about following Christ?

_____

_____

How is my personal life and ministry doing in relation to the "Irreducible Core" of loving God, loving others and making disciples as a way of life?

_____

_____

Evaluate

What needs to change in my life and ministry to line up with the IC?

_____

_____

Adjust

How can I best make those changes?

_____

_____

Do

What are my next steps to come into that alignment?

_____

_____

the Message
of the kingdom

A Message from His Heart

The Gospel message, the Good News, the *Euangélion*, is a message right from the heart of God, and it's a message of love. It's about a holy love for Himself in that the Gospel is about Him reconciling all things to Himself, putting down the rebellion of angels and men (Colossians 1:19-20). It's about a love for His creation, reclaiming it all so that it might become fully what He has always intended it to be (Romans 8:19-22). It's about a love for the highest order of that creation - humanity - which bears His image, His children which He seeks to re-gather to Himself (John 3:16-17). It is about His love that transforms us. Having loved us with everything He is, we can respond and love Him with everything we are (1 John 4:19, Matthew 22:34-40) be empowered to love others, giving away that self-same love to others (Matthew 28:18-20). The Gospel message is all about His heart - He who *is* love.

That redemptive love took shape in two forms when it entered our reality of time-space: the incarnation in the Son of Man, Jesus Christ; and the Kingdom of God which the Son both brought and proclaimed. Christ the King, both ruler of the Kingdom and doorway to the Kingdom, came into this "world" to retake that which was lost in the rebellion: *"The reason the Son of God appeared was to destroy the works of the devil"* (1 John 3:8b).

This kingdom (in Greek *basilia* - royal dominion, sovereignty, right to rule over a specific territory) was the place/state of being where liberated and reconciled creation could once again bask in the glow of the Father's love. Humanity, as the highest order of all creation, enjoys the greatest fruit of His Kingdom rule - what we call salvation or eternal life. It is precisely because Christ rules that we are saved, as there is no salvation without His dominion over sin, over the flesh, over even death itself. Our salvation is the blessed benefit of His dominion in our lives:

The Spirit of the Lord is upon me,
because he has anointed me
to proclaim good news to the poor.
He has sent me to proclaim liberty to the captives
and recovering of sight to the blind,
to set at liberty those who are oppressed,
to proclaim the year of the Lord's favor. (Luke 4:18-19)

Hope, liberation, wholeness, healing, freedom, forgiveness - all words of love, all words describing His kingdom, all words from His heart. This message of love, this message from His heart to ours, is the message of His Kingdom. Jesus came to embody this kingdom (literally), to proclaim it though His words (illumination) and His works of power (illustration), and to usher in the beginning of God's kingdom rule in the Earth, of which we are both the beneficiaries and the ones through whom He continues His Kingdom-extending work. Let's look at it more in-depth, as this too is a central issue to our organic reformation.

The Message of the Kingdom: Euangélion

When most people hear the word "marathon" they think of a race run annually in many cities around the world, one which is precisely 26 miles, 365 yards in length (or duration, depending how you look at it!). Before Marathon was a race, it was a place, where in 490 BC a decisive battle was won - a watershed in the Greco-Persian War. Legend has it that a Greek soldier, Pheidippides, ran from Marathon to Athens (you guessed it - just over 26 miles) with the good news of the victory - and then dropped dead on the spot. The message he carried was the *euangélion (u-on-gellee-on)*, the good news of the victory over the Persians.

This term was the Greek phrase used by the writers of the New Testament for the word we now know as "gospel," the Old English translation of the word from "God spell". It was a term that had political ramifications, used by the Greeks and later the Romans (who stole everything Greek, even their country) to refer to a message of great joy that brought news of a military victory that either ensured the continuance of the current ruling order, or the establishment of a new one (depending which side you were on!) In scripture you see this in several familiar passages:

> *How beautiful upon the mountains*
> *are the feet of him who brings good news,*
> *who publishes peace, who brings good news of happiness,*
> *who publishes salvation,*
> *who says to Zion, "Your God reigns."* (Isaiah 52:7)

It was a good thing when it was said that the herald is coming with great joy! It meant that things were going to be OK - your king won the day, and his reign was continued or extended. Peace was now going to be a reality because the enemies of that peace and way of life had now been subdued.

Such a message of hope was sometimes also proclaimed at the birth of a new emperor, indicating the continuance of peaceful rule, and accompanied by great rejoicing. We see this scene played out with an angelic runner coming from heaven announcing the birth of a new Universal Emperor, Jesus Christ the Son of God:

> *And in the same region there were shepherds out in the field, keeping watch over their flock by night. And an angel of the Lord appeared to them, and the glory of the Lord shone around them, and they were filled with fear. And the angel said to them, "Fear not, for behold, I bring you good news of a great joy that will be for all the people. For unto you is born this day in the city of David a Savior, who is Christ the Lord.* (Luke 2:8-11)

The word here again for "good news" is *euangélion*, with this heavenly herald announcing the coming of God's dominion through the birth of the Davidic Messiah. The angels were saying that through the birth of this new king there is a new government coming, so rejoice! The shepherds would all have known the politically charged meaning of the term, both from the Scripture and the Roman-dominated culture of their day.

It is this message of the Kingdom of God that Jesus comes proclaiming, both in word and deed:

> *Now after John was arrested, Jesus came into Galilee, proclaiming the gospel of God, and saying, "The time is fulfilled, and the kingdom of God is at hand; repent and believe in the gospel."* (Mark 1:14-15)

Jesus came declaring that *basilia*, or God's sovereign dominion, and that such a dominion was good news of liberation and freedom, good news of a new order that was emerging. He called His hearers to believe in (not simply the existence of) this new Kingdom order. The word used is *pisteuo* - to be convinced in such a way as to rely upon, having enough confidence in it to act or be willing to act upon it (our definition). The call is not for His followers just to believe that He is the Messiah, but to trust in His Kingdom, His dominion, His ability to rule in their lives for their benefit, to base their lives on it. One is a mental assent to a fact, the other is a *posture of life*. Faith includes a mental assent to truth. Biblical faith is mental assent to the Truth, Jesus, that which you base your life upon. The Apostle Paul highlights this when writing to the early church in Rome, some of whom were in Caesars' direct service.

> *because, if you confess with your mouth that Jesus is Lord and believe in your heart that God raised him from the dead, you will be saved. For with the heart one believes and is justified, and with the mouth one confesses and is saved.* (Romans 10:9-10)

When we closely compare the "good news" of the Caesar cult with Paul's words in Romans, we see a deliberate parody of the pagan message. Paul's readers in Rome must have understood this, and he must have intended them to.

In the days of the New Testament, the cult of Caesar was the fastest-growing religion in the Mediterranean world. The emperors of Rome did not claim full divine honors, but they did adopt the title "son of god". Of course, the god in question was their recently deceased, and newly deified, predecessor. And in the provinces, from Greece and Turkey through the Middle East to Egypt, divinization was standard. The logic was simple. People had worshiped rulers before; why shouldn't Augustus and his successors, with their extraordinary powers, receive the same divine honors?

As the imperial cult grew, the proclamation of hope and a promised future grew with it. This proclamation or "good news" was that Caesar, the son of God, was now the lord of the whole world, claiming allegiance from everybody in return for bringing salvation and justice to the world. Obedient and faithful response to the cult and its deified leader was expected. Resistance was met with crucifixion. The system was based on sheer power.

When we view the New Testament in this light, the power of the Gospel and the Kingdom that was ushered in by Christ becomes all the more significant. More specifically, when Paul wrote Romans he wasn't offering a benign religion or faith detached from the world of Roman power. He was confronting imperial power head-on with a bold and redemptive faith based in the true King.

In the opening lines of his letter to the Romans (1:1-17), Paul announces that he is coming to Rome as the messenger bearing God's "good news," the news about His son, the royal heir of David (in Psalms, the Davidic king would rule the whole world). In this light, we see that "Jesus is Lord" is parallel to the Roman political term "Caesar is Lord." Thus, in "confess[ing] with your mouth," you swear a new allegiance to the one true King, Jesus. In this phrase - Jesus is Lord - the writers of the New Testament co-opted a phrase that was packed with political innuendo. Commonly known to the citizens of the Roman Empire of the day, it was in usage as part of the deification and worship of Caesar as a god. Here Paul challenges them to make their allegiance to the One True God, Jesus, and to trust in His power as King to rule even over their deaths.

The resurrection marked Jesus as God's son - the one and true King and Lord of the Universe - and as such He is claiming allegiance from Jew and gentile alike. The resurrection is proof of God's dominion, and "believing in your heart" is expressing trust in His Kingdom rule. Although Roman Christians understood this switch of allegiance ("Caesar is Lord" to "Jesus is Lord") could cost them their lives; Christ's Kingdom even ruled over death itself. Paul was saying that Christian discipleship is about what *you rely upon*. As disciples, Jesus is calling us to rely upon nothing other than the Kingdom rule of God as expressed in Himself.

Paul was not ashamed of this "good news," and was willing to be the runner announcing Jesus as the risen Messiah and Lord, the one true God, the "good news" that unveils salvation and justice for the whole world. There is one King, and He has come in Jesus. His Kingdom is here and His rule is present.

The gospel / good news (euangélion) is the gospel of the Kingdom of God, *not* just of human salvation. Human redemption is part of the Kingdom emergence, and is a blessed outcome of Kingdom rule (see Luke 4:16-21) - it is not the universal focus, but rather the centrality around the Kingdom rule being reestablished is the focus. God Himself is the center of the Kingdom. Missing this seminal issue has led the Church in the West astray. The human-centric tendencies of such a gospel leaves us with a false assurance of eternity as it is devoid of the radical demands of the Lordship of Christ. John Wimber, founder of the Vineyard movement, often said that such a Gospel produced "saved, selfish people." In other words, saved people who may have some form of belief in Christ, but have not surrendered to the radical demands of His Kingdom.

In the Mark 1 passage, Jesus calls His hearers (and us) to *repent* (in Greek *metánoia* - to completely change direction through a change of heart and mind). He calls for a total reorientation of what one relies upon. Your reliance is no longer on yourself, but on the Kingdom rule of God. Therefore, life is not lived in your power, but in His. Our heart, mind and priorities are now reformed around the Kingdom: *"But seek first the kingdom of God and his righteousness, and all these things will be added to you"* (Matthew 6:33).

The call is to also trust in a transcendent Kingdom - the Kingdom of God, or the Kingdom of Heaven as the terms are used interchangeably in the Gospels. His kingdom is transcendent - not of the fallen, corrupt universe (Greek cosmos - world order) as we see in His dialog with Pontius Pilate:

> *So Pilate entered his headquarters again and called Jesus and said to him, "Are you the King of the Jews?" Jesus answered, "Do you say this of your own accord, or did others say it to you about me?" Pilate answered, "Am I a Jew? Your own nation and the chief priests have delivered you over to me. What have you done?" Jesus answered, "My kingdom is not of this world. If my kingdom were of this world, my servants would have been fighting, that I might not be delivered over to the Jews. But my kingdom is not from the world." Then Pilate said to him, "So you are a king?" Jesus answered, "You say that I am a king. For this purpose I was born and for this purpose I have come into the world - to bear witness to the truth. Everyone who is of the truth listens to my voice." Pilate said to him, "What is truth?" After he had said this, he went back outside to the Jews and told them, "I find no guilt in him."* (John 18:33-38)

Brought up on charges of sedition against the Empire (Jesus and His followers *were* proclaiming a euangélion, after all), Jesus tells Pilate that His Kingdom is unlike anything he has seen in the Empire, that it is not of the sinful, fallen nature of this world order, but transcends time-space and is pure, based in truth. Pilate himself realizes that Jesus is not seditious in the human sense, but is speaking of higher things. Jesus senses this openness in Pilate, but Pilate ends the dialog seeking to release Him.

Pilate had his "*kairos* moment" - his *specially appointed time* - and missed it. Again in Mark 1, Jesus said that the Kingdom of God was now emerging in our universe, and people need to respond through repentance and trust, that the *kairos* was now, and demanded a response. There was a "fullness" of time for the Kingdom to *emerge*. We are still in that *kairos* time - now is the day of *salvation* (2 Corinthians 6:2). The time for the Kingdom to emerge in our lives is now. For the Church in the West, the time for us to embrace the revolutionary message of the euangélion is now. And while there is a future point when the Kingdom will come in its fullness (Revelation 11:15), we must embrace the demands of the Kingdom and its King now. All of this is reflected rather clearly in the

Great Commission when Christ tells us to "teach them to observe all that I have commanded you." (Matthew 28:20)

Ministering the Message of the Kingdom

Why is an understanding of the gospel message so important to the Organic Reformation? Fundamentally, it is because the Church in the West, to a great degree, has shifted the emphasis of the Gospel away from the King and His Kingdom, and towards the Kingdom benefit for humanity. This is not to suggest there are not benefits as there are many. We have instead nullified the *call to discipleship* by substituting a *call to belief and attendance*. In the West, Christianity has become a *belief system*, not *a way of life*. Easily compartmentalized, such religion is a band-aid for the soul but cannot cure the spiritual cancer inside each one of us. Jesus, the Ultimate Rabbi, came that we might have life, and have it in abundance, to the full. The call to the Kingdom is a revolutionary call to radical obedience through radical surrender of our hearts to His heart. That surrender, the *metánoia* Jesus speaks of, must be played out through all of life, a life permeated by the Kingdom, expressing the Kingdom, extending the Kingdom, displayed as a witness to the transforming love and power of King Jesus.

Another reason a proper understanding of the Gospel message is important in this Organic Reformation is that we have left the *full proclamation* of this Gospel for the simple preaching of its tenets. We have exchanged the Person of the King for propositional statements about Him, switching from transformational encounter with the Living God to knowing a whole lot of stuff about Him. We have mistakenly believed that knowing a whole lot about God will bring us into a vital relationship with Him, that belief is simply mentally assenting to the truthfulness of scriptural propositional statements. Nothing could be further from the truth - the demons believe, but they shudder in fear (James 2:19). Belief is not faith, as faith requires action and always involves risk. Faith - *pisteuo* - that trusting in, that relying upon, is demonstrated in a life lived out unto God. Acquisition of information alone will not produce that, nor will simply listening to preaching. Information is necessary, impartation is critical and incarnation is a must. Incarnation is the evidence or fruit that transformation has taken place. There must be an encounter with Him that transforms.

Paul said,

For I will not venture to speak of anything except what Christ has accomplished through me to bring the Gentiles to obedience-by word and deed, by the power of signs and wonders, by the power of the Spirit of God-so that from Jerusalem and all the way around to Illyricum I have fulfilled the ministry of the gospel of Christ; (Romans 15:18-19)

Here Paul said that he fulfilled the ministry of the gospel, or fully proclaimed it through his words (teaching/preaching), his deeds (the way he lived among them), and the miraculous signs and wonders demonstrating the dominion of the Kingdom, all of which was empowered by the Holy Spirit. We, unlike Paul, for the most part have focused on the preaching and teaching, believing that methodology was sufficient in and of itself to bring transformation. But Paul says there is more. Yes, preaching and teaching, but also the modeling of life in Christ (see 1 Corinthians 11:1) and the working of the Spirit in power through Him. Indeed today, in places around the globe where Christianity is growing, all three things tend to be present - the preaching of the Gospel of the Kingdom, combined with the living of a Kingdom-centric life by those who minister, and the demonstration of the Spirit and of power (see 1 Corinthians 2:1-5). This is the full proclamation of the Gospel of the Kingdom (Romans 15:18); in word, in life and in the power of the Spirit, all producing a powerful encounter with the powerful King of Kings and Lord of Lords, Jesus Christ.

So how then do we minister the message of the Kingdom? How do we fully proclaim this mystery of Christ? Well, first of all we have to remember that this is a message from His heart, a message of grace: *"Fear not, little flock, for it is your Father's good pleasure to give you the kingdom"* (Luke 12:32). The Kingdom rule of God is a gift given by Himself to humanity through His Son. It is received by an active faith - a life lived out - which leads us to loving obedience. His heart impacts our heart, and changes us, empowering us to love Him in return (1 John 4:19), which overflows into loving others. The message must be rooted in this love and grace, because the demands are so huge:

> *"Do not think that I have come to bring peace to the earth. I have not come to bring peace, but a sword. For I have come to set a man against his father, and a daughter against her mother, and a daughter-in-law against her mother-in-law. And a person's enemies will be those of his own household. Whoever loves father or mother more than me is not worthy of me, and whoever loves son or daughter more than me is not worthy of me. And whoever does not take his cross and follow me is not worthy of me. Whoever finds his life will lose it, and whoever loses his life for my sake will find it.* (Matthew 10:34-39)

It was quite common for a rabbi in Jesus' day to make such demands of His disciples, placing devotion to the master teacher and his teaching above even one's own life and family. The imagery of the Cross says that following Him will be a costly choice made daily. But the demands of the Kingdom upon the disciple of Jesus are only in proportion to the Gift that has been given. We continue to offer the cheap, unsanctified grace which Dietrich Bonheoffer so decried in his generation, falling in line with the humanistic, consumer-driven Western worldview, relinquishing the loving demands of the Kingdom in an effort to gain believers and attendees. In this we both forsake the love of God and His calling to make disciples, settling instead for weekly meetings full of those seeking spiritual fulfillment through entertainment. We default to the circus.

We also have to remember that for those who have trusted in Christ, we have already entered the Kingdom: *"He has delivered us from the domain of darkness and transferred us to the kingdom of his beloved Son, in whom we have redemption, the forgiveness of sins"* (Colossians 1:13-14). Many who have been brought into the Kingdom in the West are positionally and salvifically in the Kingdom, but walk daily under the dominion of darkness. Through our incomplete presentation of the gospel, we have left people disempowered and unprepared for life in the Kingdom. As a result, many struggle and even fall away. This may be one of the primary reasons why the "sin stats" in the Church are pretty much the same as those in the world; they have not been given a Kingdom worldview as a perspective on reality nor a Kingdom lifestyle as a model for their own. Additionally, most have never seen a miraculous demonstration of God's dominion and power. And we wonder why we are in the state we are in. This is not God's heart, and if His Kingdom message is one of love, grace, freedom, wholeness, righteous, peace and joy, we have done little to embody this or bring such a reality to the people in our churches. For this we must repent, as the Gospel of the Kingdom is so much more than we have made it out to be!

Simply put, the return to the centrality of the Kingdom causes us to shed all the machinery of ministry and religion which has become encrusted on the proclamation of the Gospel over the past 2,000 years. We are mindful of and grateful for all we have gained through the historic Church and enjoy the benefit of it today. The Organic Reformation is a call to go back before all that, to the Author and Finisher of our faith (Hebrews 12:2), to the simplicity of the radical love of the Father, and the radical call to this Kingdom of love and grace, to the core of Jesus' teaching - lived out everywhere, not compartmentalized, with no caveats. We need to return to the life-on-life process of Jesus as well as the centrality of the Kingdom in our life and ministry.

Responding to the Message

Each of us must first personally and individually respond to the Gospel of the Kingdom before we can minister it to others, not just in the sense of salvation, but to its demands and to the fullness of its ministry. Here is what it says to each of us, from Jesus' words in Mark 1:14-15, "Now after John was arrested, Jesus came into Galilee, proclaiming the gospel of God, and saying, "The time is fulfilled, and the kingdom of God is at hand; repent and believe in the gospel."

There is a new governing order emerging in our universe. We *must* surrender to it *and* rely upon it. To come *to this reliance on the new order* we must release our reliance on the old order, which was ruled by self. We must completely change: our direction, our heart, our thinking, our way of life, our priorities, our perception of reality - *we must be re-made*. The only way this can happen is to embrace this new order of God's dominion, even unto death, surrendering everything to the King of Kings. The territory He wants is our hearts, and ultimately, all of the created order. Now is the time for us to surrender to the Kingdom rule of God in our lives. Now is the time for the Kingdom order to emerge in our churches.

What will this all look like in our lives and the lives of those disciples we are making for Jesus? The hallmark of a Kingdom-oriented disciple, one that has been impacted by the euangélion, is that they are living the "irreducible core" of loving God with everything they are, loving and serving others in every way they can, and making disciples everywhere they go, all the time. There are verifiable outcomes in the life of a disciple which Bill Hull (taken from *Choose the Life* 14) describes as:

> *Believe what Jesus believed (transformed mind). Faith requires that I believe what Jesus believed and the life He taught, particularly in the Sermon on the Mount, is possible now. For this transformation of the mind to happen we need to commit to listen to the voice of God through prayer, study of His Word, and meditation and reflection in order to better hear His voice and transform our minds. A transformation that impacts my lifestyle.*

> *Live as Jesus lived (transformed character). Faith cannot be faith unless we base our lives on it. To simply believe in something to be true is not the same, as noted above, in basing one's life on it. This belief must impact behavior, transforming our character in such a way that we bear fruit (Galatians 5:22-23).*

> *Love as Jesus loved (transformed relationships). If we are living the transformed life, then the love that transforms should be the basis and foundation by which we live (John 13:34-35). We are called to love each other as He has loved us (John 15:12). This is not a love that is preferential, loving only those that love in return, but incarnational and intentional, motivated by the heart of Christ that is now in us (Galatians 2:20). What concerns God concerns us; what God loves, we love.*

> *Minister as Jesus ministered (transformed service). Scripture makes it clear that the heart of our King is one of servanthood (Mark 10:45). Love has two distinct elements to it. Love gives and love forgives. One of the greatest*

tests of a servant heart is how we respond in our heart when we are actually treated like a servant. For the servant heart, it is not an issue, but for the person who is acting like a servant (doing acts with self-centered motivations), then being treated as such will cause offense or hurt. Please keep in mind that we are not condoning being treated as nothing - kindness and the valuing and re-valuing of the other is critical to living lives that honor the Imago Dei, even if severely diminished, in others. Our point is a simple one that deals with heart attitude. Love longs to give and this giving is powerfully demonstrated in the servant life of the King of Kings.

Lead as Jesus led (transformed influence). Living and leading like Jesus invites the leader into a life of "irrelevance" (Henri Nouwen). "Irrelevance" being represented in our values of servanthood, humility, sacrifice, and love in contrast to self-gain, self-aggrandizement, giving to get, and love where it benefits me. We spend too much time trying to be relevant in the wrong places, resulting in a relevance that supports the values of the world more than the values of the Kingdom of God. If we are leading as Jesus led then our influence seeks to create an environment where the Holy Spirit can transform character and heart; where the love of the Kingdom is released in individuals, resulting in sacrifice, giving, and forgiving. It means that we weep on Thursday for our neighbors and friends that do not know the love and grace of our Jesus. That we no longer weep on Monday because our attendance and tithes were low. It means we return to the values of our King and His Kingdom and lead His people with His heart and in His way. Developing a people that are full of love reflected most clearly in the Fruit of the Spirit, a people captured by a love that brings freedom, broken for a lost people and moved by that love to help the lost find their way home, strengthened with purpose and clarity that restores the Imago Dei and creation; a people that live as light and salt, releasing and preserving life in every venue and in every way; a people that that live in harmony with the Creator of the Universe and in harmony with themselves and each other - you know a taste of heaven - the appetizer in this life that tells us there is something so magnificent yet to come. The meal is on its way - may we lead our people in such a way that reflects the fullness of our King and His Kingdom!

So, there are verifiable outcomes in the life of the disciples of Jesus, which Kingdom ministry will produce out of the way of life Jesus calls us to, teaches us about and leads us in each day. The ministry of the Gospel of the Kingdom will produce fruit when done in its completeness, with His heart of love and grace. Again, that fruit is an organic outcome of a life-process, which we see wonderfully displayed in the life of the early Kingdom community in Acts 2:27, "praising God and having favor with all the people. And the Lord added to their number day by day those who were being saved."

Such fruit is an outcome of Kingdom life and ministry. Such fruit is the goal of the Organic Reformation.

Reflect

Why is it important to understand that the Gospel of the Kingdom is *Christ-centered* not *human-centered?*

_____

_____

Evaluate

How does true *metánoia* (repentance), as defined here, place the demands of the Kingdom upon our lives?

_____

_____

Why must the message of the Kingdom be preached both with words and works?

_____

_____

How does all this affect what we call "ministry?"

_____

_____

Adjust

What needs to come in line with the Kingdom: In your thinking? Your lifestyle? Your ministry practice?

_____

_____

Do

What do you need to do next to make these adjustments? List them.

_____

_____

the Way
of the kingdom

The Rabbinical Process of Jesus

Ministry is about making disciples, and the work of the ministry is spiritual formation - seeing Christ formed in others (Galatians 4:19). Whatever we are attempting to facilitate in our ecclesiological realm, the outcome of that facilitation needs to be oriented to forming Christ in others. More simply, it is about discipleship. Within our Western worldview, we have a myriad of processes for discipleship and many programs and curricula that could be accessed to help us in our endeavor. All of these are well intentioned, and many are excellent. Before you decide on one curriculum or process over another and go on a discipleship shopping spree, let us take a moment to introduce you to the rabbinical process of Jesus as the basis and framework for discipleship.

Before we talk about the rabbinical process of Jesus, let us take a moment to talk about framework. One of the key pastoral issues we have noticed is that pastors often lack a working framework for life and ministry. Many do not have a clear and operational philosophy of ministry that frames who they are and what they do. As a result, like a house that lacks the frame, many ministries lack the frame by which to build. What this results in is the need to buy off the shelf frameworks and processes that are fully packaged. Nothing wrong, necessarily, with the off the shelf products, but they may not have the framework that is most conducive to who you are, the values you live, the vision that God has given you and the spiritual community you work with. We then have to sort through the material to pick and choose what works for us and what doesn't. Occasionally it works wonderfully because there is a similar DNA between the ministries.

All of that to say, pastors and leaders need a simple framework, not an ecclesiological framework that is often steeped in a prescribed and interpreted tradition shaped by a Western mindset/worldview. You know, Western traditions that are more focused on form than on the simplicity of being followers of Christ as a spiritual community called the Church.

The Irreducible Core (IC) functions as a powerful and simple framework that allows every pastor and leader to frame their ministry around the heart of Jesus. The beauty of the IC is that it can flex into a myriad of traditions and forms and still be the IC. The heart of the Church is then the same, our expressions and forms may vary, as they should, but the heart should be the same as that of the One we call God. How we live out the IC and incarnate it will be determined by how God has made us, the call He has placed in our lives, the vision He has given us, the leadership community and their giftings, the tradition or tribe to which we belong, and the community to which we have been called.

The rabbinical process of Christ is not set on a methodology or propositional construct (although propositions are involved). In the West, we tend to focus on the doctrine basis (proposition) and the methodology rather than the relationship that is the necessary ingredient for discipleship to take place. When Jesus called His disciples, He called them to Himself: "Come follow Me" (Matthew 4:19). This was not a call to a persuasion or a new practice or methodology, but a call to a person and a way of life. To answer this call for the disciples would mean a re-orientation of their lives to the rabbi and his interpretation or yoke of the Torah. This interpretation would require the disciples to live within the worldview or framework lived and taught by the rabbi. The disciple were eager to learn what the rabbi knew, to do what the rabbi did and ultimately, to become like the rabbi. This was in the heart of the early disciples as they followed Jesus, their Rabbi. *The Ethics of the Fathers* echoes this sentiment as the wise sage writes, "...cover yourself with the dust of their (Rabbi) feet, and drink in their words with thirst" (cited by Young 122).

Jesus is a first century rabbi, functioning within the reality of Judaism as one whose heart is set on fulfilling the Torah in every way that God, the Father, originally intended. Jesus did not come to abolish or destroy the Torah but to fulfill it (Matthew 5:17-18) and show the world what it looks like to be a true Jew that is in pure relationship with God as revealed and instructed in the Torah. Jesus speaks as in insider that is seeking to reform the heart of His people so that they might return to the purity of what God intended. Jesus' yoke is then simplified as He boldly declares that all the Law and Prophets "hang on" or "depend on" two simple commands: "..."You shall love the Lord your God with all your heart and with all your soul and with all your mind. This is the great and first commandment. And a second is like it: You shall love your neighbor as yourself" (Matthew 22:37-39).

The Jewish work, *The Ethics of the Fathers*, illustrates this reality of love. "Hillel said, 'Be of the disciples of Aaron, loving peace and pursuing peace, loving every single person, and drawing each one near to the Torah'" (cited in Young 123). The essence of life for Jesus was housed in a relationship of love with the Father that expressed itself in love for oneself and love for others. This is precisely why Jesus added a new commandment for His disciples that verified whose disciples they were. Jesus commanded them (and us), "...that you love one another: just as I have loved you, you also are to love one another. By this all people will know that you are my disciples, if you have love for one another" (John 13:34-35).The verification of our discipleship or whose Rabbi we belong to is our love for one another.

Of course, in the world of ecclesiological practice and theology, if you don't agree with someone then you don't have to love them. Well, maybe that's too harsh. We at least don't have to fellowship with them anymore because we are not on the same page. We realize that is not what they may say, but it is what they often do. Church is often like two families arguing over which vehicle to take on a trip. One family wants to take the RV and the other wants to take the SUV. In their argument they lose sight of the purpose and destination, and focus only on the reasons their vehicle of choice is superior and more necessary. The point of the trip, family fun and togetherness, is lost in the heated exchange and both families will not budge. The argument for the RV is that there is more room, people can rest better and relax while we drive and we can interact better as a family. The argument for the SUV is that it is roomy enough, gets better gas mileage, is easier to drive, is less likely to get into an accident and is easier to park. The families can't agree on the mode of transportation, the "how," and so they take separate vehicles, no longer able to vacation together. How unfortunate! How silly! How like the Church.

The Apostle Paul's exhortation in Philippians 1:27 is for uniform direction, a common mind, and unity of thought and will. To be worthy of the gospel of Christ requires that we stand firm...

> *...in one spirit*
> *...with one mind (one purpose)*
> *...striving side by side*

It is so easy as the church to get sidetracked and spend more time disagreeing over the "how" of doing ministry that we lose focus on the "what" of ministry, or our destination. The "how" has become more significant than the purpose. So it is with us, our thinking and striving about the "how" cannot be seen in isolation from the overall purpose of our lives. What frames our life and ministry is not always embodied in what we say, but it is clearly expressed in what we do. So, as individuals and as churches we can lose sight of our ultimate purpose and destination, which is to love God with all that we are, love others even as we love ourselves, and make disciples, becoming entangled by focusing too much on the means. That we get to this three-fold goal is that which is important, not how we get there.

You know, when your political party determines your theology, when you base your Biblical views more on the Constitution than Scripture, when you turn Christianity into creeds and doctrines at the expense of a relationship with God, when love becomes a tool to evangelize instead of a way of life, when our denominational preference supersedes Scripture - we become "religianity" rather than being simple followers of Christ that seek to love because we have been loved (I John 4:19).

The rabbis of Jesus' day said something similar. Hillel was approached by a would-be convert that made the rather odd request, "I will believe in the God of Israel and abandon idolatry on the condition that you teach me the whole Torah while standing on one foot." Hillel answered with grace and dignity as he instructed this potential disciple with these brilliant words, "What you do not want someone to do to you, do not do to him or her. The rest of the Torah is commentary upon this principle. Now go and learn it!" (cited in Young 193)

Enough of our ecclesiological rambling - let's get back to our Rabbi Jesus

The discipleship process of Jesus finds its basis in the promise of Mark 1:17 as it anticipates the disciples' new vocation as "fishers of men" rather than mere students of the Law. The disciples would ultimately share in the ministry of Jesus and eventually continue and multiply it rather than simply being proponents of the Law. This is the key to the relational rabbinic process as embodied by Jesus, distinguishing Him from the rabbis of the day: Jesus was calling these men to Himself as the Way, the Truth and the Life, and not just to the teaching of Torah. In Jesus' day, it was common for a young and eager student to seek out a rabbi and ask to become his disciple. The rabbis were the most revered individuals within Jewish culture and to become a disciple of a rabbi was like being accepted into Harvard or some prestigious place where only the best of the best get to go. To be able to say that you are a disciple of Rabbi such and such was a great privilege, honor and desired outcome. Not all, however, were able to become disciples of a rabbi. Many entered their family business or trade, like James and John (Matthew 4:21), in order to work, providing food and shelter for their families.

Jesus subverts this order: The disciple does not seek out the master, but is sought out by the master Himself. Jesus comes on the scene as the central figure who is a Rabbi like no other. He does not wait for the disciples to seek Him out. He seeks out His disciples and calls them to Himself. In answering the call the disciples respond negatively and positively to the call of Jesus. Negatively, they respond by leaving their family life and occupations. Discipleship involves leaving behind one's former life and ties - more specifically, living for the Kingdom of God. Positively, they follow Jesus and begin to learn what it means to orient their lives upon the interpretation/yoke of their Rabbi as He leads them into life in the Kingdom of God.

One must keep in mind that all through this process one must be sure to make disciples as you go - evangelize and gather into the Kingdom community as you live life. Discipleship is more than a program; it is a way of life that is lived out from the inside out. As a matter of fact, the imperative in the Great Commission is not, "go," but "make disciples". The great evangelical heresy is that we place the emphasis on going and not on what Jesus said - making disciples. Please know, we are grateful that people go and believe people should as we take the Gospel to the world. As long as we are making disciples, the going is good.

Oswald Chambers enriches us with his insight, "Jesus did not say, 'Go and discourse about making disciples,' but 'Go and *make* disciples.' The making of converts is a Satanic perversion of this strenuous workmanlike product. How many make followers of their own convictions, and how few make disciples! The production of saints, that is the work. God Almighty regenerates men's souls; we make disciples. Are we doing it? God is apparently not very careful whom He uses or what He uses for the work of regeneration; but none but the master workmen, that is, the saints, can make disciples. Does your work for God stamp the hearts of the people round about you with an enervating, sentimental love for you? Or does every remembrance of you cause a strenuous stirring of hearts to do better, grander work for God?" (329)

The purpose of discipleship is to help people grow deeper in their relationship with God, to be shaped into the image of Christ, discovering who they are as sons and daughters of God, and their role as servants and stewards in the Kingdom. Bill Hull provides 5 stages of discipleship.

A disciple submits to a teacher who teaches him or her how to follow Jesus
A disciple learns Jesus' words
A disciple learns Jesus' way of ministry
A disciple imitates Jesus' life and character
A disciple finds and teaches other disciples for Jesus (36)

Hull provides some excellent commentary as he analyzes the common church practice of discipleship and concludes that churches generally do three of the five principles. A small minority do four of the five, and almost none do all five. Here are the three most common that churches employ when it comes to discipleship:

A disciple learns Jesus' words
A disciple learns Jesus' way of ministry
A disciple imitates Jesus' life and character

The above three are the easiest to do. They are the least challenging and realistically can be done without having to change. There is something about submitting yourself to the authority of Christ in another person that provides the necessary environment for transformation to take place. When we are submitted to the authority of Christ in another person, as well as finding and developing our own disciples, we find the prime setting for personal transformation and true incarnational discipleship.

All this to say - the *relationship* is the key vehicle by which the discipleship process is engaged. When we view the ontological reality of the Trinity, (as God the Father, God the Son and God the Spirit) who relate in this dance of love, we see how this portrays the intimacy and pure reciprocity (*perichoresis*) of their relationship. This ontological understanding does not result in confusion or loss of identity amongst the Father, Son and Spirit. God exists in relationship with Himself and creation and this dance is the pattern by which this three-Person life is to be lived out in each of us. Discipleship allows us to discover the beauty of both mutuality and individuality. This beautiful tension is expressed most prolifically in this community of being, in which each person, while maintaining their distinctive identity, penetrates the others and is penetrated by them. Without relational submission to the authority of Christ in others, something of the Imago Dei, our full humanity will never be achieved as God has designed. Humanity cannot be programmed into a person nor can it be programmed out. Humanity is released and finds its full expression in the relational dance with God the Father as it is incarnated in the life of another human being. We are in dire need of growing close to the Person of Christ and incarnating His presence and Person to a lost and dying world that longs to join a dance of love that results in the discovery of self (identity), the love of others and the realization of our purpose and destiny in the Father's Kingdom.

Life-pattern Teaching

Jesus lays out for us the process by which discipleship is most effectively engaged - life-pattern teaching. Jesus lived in community (a shared life together) with His disciples. This "life-on-life" is the essence of organic life and ministry. The term "organic" can most simply defined as "life-on-life", or "life that gives birth to life". Jesus incarnated/embodied the presence of the Father in His life (John 1:14; Hebrews 1:1-3) and imparted this life to others through the vehicle of relationship. The relational means by which this life was transmitted was in an encounter with the Way, the Truth and the Life. The disciple-making process is still the same today. People encounter Jesus through His Church - His body - the fullness of Him that fills everything in every way (Ephesians 1:23). It is this relational dynamic, this incarnational reality that makes the whole process organic. It is not mechanized, and although it may embrace a form or a process, it is ultimately about seeing Christ formed in others. Jesus showed His disciples who the Father was both in word and deed - all ministry is ultimately, revelation based (Spirit-driven) and incarnational.

Theology is more descriptive than prescriptive. We describe, through the written Word what has happened to us in our encounter with the God of the universe. Since Jesus is the Word (John 1:14), we need to have an encounter or experience with the Living Word before we can understand fully and spiritually the literal words of the Bible (I Corinthians 2:10-14). Such an encounter is an embarrassment to the modern mind. We don't like to have things in our lives that we cannot compartmentalize. After experiencing the mystery of such an encounter, the great Roman Catholic theologian, Thomas Aquinas wrote in his *Summa Theologica*, "I can write no more for everything I have written is straw."

Ministry is not simply about developing competencies, or what we call "discipleship to task", but about spirituality, a way of life, what we call "discipleship to character". The apostle Paul said, "Be imitators of me, as I am of Christ" (I Corinthians 11:1). Ministry is not only about what we say, but also about what we do. Our words should simply compliment the reality of our lives. As pastors and leaders we are to incarnate or show our people the way of Christianity through "life-pattern teaching." In that sense, we are the life pattern as we follow the Life Pattern (Jesus). Jesus is not only the Way to the Father, but the "Way" for life - the pattern by which we live as we are empowered by the Holy Spirit to do so.

The Curriculum of Life

Jesus also makes it clear that life is the curriculum. Everything in life is used by the rabbi to shape his disciple. We learn this from His life and ministry but most poignantly on the road to Emmaus (Luke 24:13-32). The narrative in this passage paints a powerful picture of the nature of our discipleship process. Jesus meets Cleopas and an unidentified disciple on the road to Emmaus (both were possibly included in Jesus' group of 70 disciples). Jesus engages the two on the road, meeting them where they are. Christ clearly notices the downtrodden look on their faces and essentially asks them, "What's up?"

Their response indicates they are stunned that this guy did not know what had transpired with the crucifixion of Jesus. They journey with Jesus and He dialogues with them, utilizing Scripture in the conversation to explain the happenings of the past three days. As the dinner hour approached, they invite Jesus to dinner and at the breaking of bread, their eyes are opened and they realize it is Jesus. It is at this point that Jesus disappears. The two muse over what has happened and strongly conclude, "Did not our hearts burn within us while he talked to us on the road, while he opened to us the Scriptures?" (Luke 24:32)

We must first understand that the means of discipleship is peripatetic. That is to say, it involves a walk. Discipleship is essentially two people walking together, sharing over the course of months or years. It is this walk that allowed the two on the road to Emmaus to see Jesus. Discipleship is then that process or walk whereby we explicate the reality of Scripture with our lives, expounding its fullness in the day to day reality of life, leading to the disciple seeing Christ more clearly.

The curriculum that we employ is life. This is not saying that utilizing a written curriculum is wrong or unnecessary. Rather, it is to say that no matter what tool or curriculum you employ, life is the ultimate curriculum and should be where you meet people in this process. Discipleship is incarnational. Jesus met the two on the road to Emmaus where they were. Too often our discipleship processes or programs force people to come to where we are rather than the leader or rabbi going to where they are - journeying with them, living Jesus alongside them, conversing about Scripture with them as life in the Kingdom is shared and modeled. It is rather amazing to consider all the places Jesus visited and the types of people He allowed Himself to hang out with - incarnation, compelled by the love of God, will go to the highways and byways (Luke 14:23) to find the lost sons and daughters of God and let them know that there has been a place saved for them in Christ.

Focus Focus Focus

The Rabbinical process of Jesus teaches us that if you want to start an organization, make your *focus large*, on the crowd. If you want to start a movement, make your *focus small*, on the disciples or leadership community. The optimum word here is, focus. So much of our ecclesiological world has been a perfect illustration of Newton's third law of reciprocal actions which tells us that there is always an equal and opposite reaction for every force. This has resulted in an "either-or" ideology in our ecclesiological practice where the pendulum swings from one side to the other or the force of one way causes the other to react in direct opposition. This is most clearly seen in the feudal war of ecclesiological "operating systems". The first and most dominant of these "operating systems" is called "The Temple Church." In this particular system the focus is on the Sunday service and the attractional programs that this kind of church utilizes as tools in hopes of facilitating relationship. On the flip side is the "The House Church" operating system, which feels that it needs to reject all programs in an attempt to have a relational way of life. Ironically, both still prescribe something less than what the New Testament desires.

The New Testament *never directs us to a form of church* but tells us how we should relate to God and one another when we gather (Acts 2:42-47).

The early church expressed itself within the confines of first century culture which was influenced by Jewish thought and practice as well as the Gentile community that was rapidly coming to faith in Christ. This bi-polar approach to church has led to an "either-or" mentality rather than a "both-and" mindset that understands the Church to be nothing more and nothing less than Jesus plus some people that are committed to loving God, loving others and as they live life, making disciples. As we say, church can be a whole lot more than the Irreducible Core (as long as the "IC" still frames and guides the church), but it can never be any less.

We are all for any form of church that is able to express itself in a way of life around the "IC". What is essential is that any expression have at its heart the "IC", being pursued and expressed in the hearts of the individuals and families within the church and a desire to see their neighborhoods and communities impacted by the life of Christ. The form is not the issue, it is what it is at the heart of the form that matters. When a church's form is centered on the "IC" it has the potential for people to incarnate Christ within their families, neighborhoods, community, city, etc. They can live out the God-given vision housed in the leadership community. Such a leadership team, focused on living out loving God, loving others and making disciples, can empower and release the saints for the work of the ministry. The leadership, ministering from the "IC" helps people to discover their identity as sons and daughters of God, helps them to grow in Christ-likeness in the capacity of their hearts, and to engage in the pursuit of their destiny as they make their contribution to the Kingdom economy. Such a way of life allows people to grow and mature in their understanding of who they are in Christ and how they fit in His Kingdom community.

When we use the word focus, we mean precisely that. We are not suggesting that we ignore public ministry. Again, this is a "both-and" approach that allows for the Church to be all that it is, while we as leaders live out the heart of our Christ by developing incarnational discipleship pathways. Since Jesus is our model for life and ministry let's look to Him for further understanding.

Jesus ministered to the crowds in word and deed (miracles). This tells us that ministering to crowds is not wrong. There is a place for it.

Again, the key here is the focus of Jesus which was not on the crowds, but on the seventy disciples and especially on the twelve and the three. This point is most clearly demonstrated as Jesus taught the multitudes about the Kingdom, but He explained the Kingdom to His disciples. What we learn from this is that having a large or small church is not the issue. Rather the issue is our *focus* and as junior rabbis to the Senior Rabbi (Christ), we are to focus on discovering and developing disciples that live their lives around the "IC" and are dictated by the worldview of the Kingdom of God.

The focus of Christ was clearly on forming and developing His disciples for life in the Kingdom of God. As a result, Jesus taught the multitudes about the Kingdom, but He only explained the Kingdom to His disciples. Jesus' focus was not on the crowds. He did not ignore the crowds, but spent most of His time forming and developing His disciples so that they might be able to carry on what He had begun. Jesus was rather confident that His disciples would do far greater works than He (John 14:12).

The teachings of Jesus revolved around three things - all were relational - and as Martin Buber called, the "I/Thou". Jesus helped His disciples understand:

Who God was (God-awareness)
Who they were in relation to God (Self-awareness)
Who they were in relation to others (Other-awareness)

As He taught through His life as a pattern, He used both words and works to instruct about the Kingdom (John 14:12, Matthew 11:1-5), helping His disciples encounter the reality of Kingdom life and rule and what it looks like lived out in a loving relationship with God - which results in loving others as you love yourself and making disciples as you live life in His Kingdom.

Let us take a moment to define what a disciple is. Our working definition flows out of the Irreducible Core. It is someone who is growing in their devotion to:

Christ (the Person)

His Church (His People)
His Mission (His Passion)

This is the target outcome of any discipleship process or pathway. As we have said, missing one of these three elements is a "genetic defect" and can render the disciple unable to reproduce spiritually in making more disciples.

Jesus' experience shows us that there are several different types of followers, not all of which are immediately devoted disciples. So it is with us as we make disciples of Jesus today. Among those types who followed Jesus, there were the "crowd," the "casual" follower, and the committed "core." Each of these had various levels of commitment to Him, and He invested His time differently in each. Let us look at this in more detail, and how it might relate to us today.

The Crowd: Jesus ministered to crowds providing the Good News of the Kingdom in word and deed, healing the sick, casting out demons, etc. However, Jesus did not focus His ministry on the crowd. This would be analogous to worship services or celebrations in our churches today.

The Casual Christian: This is someone who honors God in name and title, but not in devotion. From the ministry of Jesus, we see that only 25% of the seed (1 in 4) grows to fruition (see Matthew 13:18-23), and in Luke 17:17, we learn that only 10%, 1 out of the 10 lepers, responds to Jesus. What we infer from this is that 10-25% of those who hear the gospel respond and grow to be fully developed disciples of Christ. What this translates into is the 20/80 reality of the modern church where 20% of the church does 80% of the work (not true in all cases but a reality that is acknowledged and verified). This also means that 75-90% of those who attend on Sunday mornings fall into these two categories of "crowd" or "casual" disciple. We are not casting a vote to do away with public services, as Jesus ministered to the crowds and so should you in whatever format you feel called to do it. Our aim here is to learn from Jesus just exactly where we should place our focus or our investment of time.

The Core: In your leadership community you will have two types of disciples: Those who are "committed" (driven by personal agenda) and those who are "devoted" (driven by the revolutionary dream of the

Kingdom). It took Jesus three years to walk with his committed group of disciples who left a great deal to follow Him. However in their faith journey with Christ it became very apparent that they each had a personal agenda. In other words, they believed that the kind of Messiah Jesus was to be was a Messiah that would come and free Israel from Roman rule and re-establish Israel in the Kingdom economy as the nation that would manifest God's glory. The disciples did not understand or believe that Jesus would go the way of the Cross, they did not comprehend the kind of Messiah He was, nor how much more He had come to do not only for Israel but the entire human race, past, present and future.

We learn from the ministry of Jesus that it takes radical, relational discipleship over a period of time (three years for Jesus' disciples) and a radical God encounter (death, resurrection and the Baptism of the Holy Spirit for the disciples to get it) to move the disciples from *committed* to *devoted.* All disciples, even radically committed followers of Christ, begin the process committed, but still possess an understanding of God too small, incomplete, or which is agenda-driven. The *process* of discipleship is what moves the disciple from being agenda-driven (committed) to Kingdom-driven (devoted). It is an issue of heart and world-view.

Circles of Relationships

So, how did Jesus make this work? How did he deal with these various groups of people and their divergent levels of commitment and devotion? Basically, we see He had various circles of relationships:

The Multitudes: These where the crowds which followed Him, for us, the congregation on Sunday.

The 72 Disciples: His rabbis in training, for us our ministry leaders/leaders in training.

The 12 Apostles: Strategic transformers

The 3 (Peter, James and John): These were His catalytic, world-changing leaders, for us it would be our pastoral staff, elders, etc.

The time investment here is the key element which brought focus to His ministry. While He *taught* the multitudes about the Kingdom, He *explained* the Kingdom to His disciples - the 3/12/72 (Matthew 13:10-11).

He spent the most time with the 3 and the 12, and the least amount time with the crowds. How opposite of our ministry time investment! Most of our week is spent preparing our sermon or managing the components for the Big Event on Sunday, with little investment in the lives of our key leadership. To be sure, Western society pushes back on our ability to be with our key leaders in the same way Jesus did, but we could do far more in re-tasking our time to invest in people whom the Lord has called to develop as His disciples.

It is important to note here that He showed an *intentional distinction* amongst these groups, giving more time to the 3 and 12 than everyone else. Why is this? Did He like them more at a personal level? No - although John thought so! It was because He recognized differing levels of Kingdom potential in each. Out of the crowds He calls His disciples (the 72/120 in the Upper Room) and gives more time to them than the multitudes. Out of this group He appoints 12 Apostles, who might be with Him more, (Mark 3:14). Among these He seems to spend more time with the three key leaders of the group, His senior apprentices with the most potential - Peter, James and John.

This is so decidedly un-Western! How dare He show favoritism amongst His followers! Very politically un-correct! Are not all Christian disciples equal? Yes, and no. Yes, all are loved equally by Jesus, all are accepted equally, all are given the same Spirit, have the same Lord, same faith, same baptism, same God and Father of them all, and are of the same One Body (Ephesians 4:5-6). But each of His followers, then and now, is graced differently (Ephesians 4:7, Romans 12:3-7) and has a different value in the Kingdom economy. (We know of Billy Graham, and we are *not* Billy Graham. We know Jack Hayford, and we are *not* Jack Hayford. Not even close!) Recognizing the difference in their potential for Kingdom extension, Jesus invested proportionally to that potential. He showed distinction for the sake of the revolution, for the work of the Kingdom. In our application, we must switch our time investment away from the crowds and to our "3 and 12," not based on personal like or dislike, but on the needs of the ongoing work of the Kingdom in and through our local church. This is the biggest organic shift most pastors and leaders will have to make. You will need to call out disciples just like Jesus did, and those who respond will need to be discerned in the Spirit as to their grace and willingness to go further in the Kingdom.

With the inner circles of the 3, the 12 and the 72, Jesus embraced a cycle of learning both relational and incarnational. He knew, as all His contemporary rabbis did, that a:

Disciple learns by hearing
Disciple learns by seeing how it is done
Disciple learns by doing it
Disciple learns by teaching it to others

We see this noted in the work of Bill Hull mentioned earlier. This requires time and space, opening our lives and ministries to those whom we should be focusing on in the first place. People have to be with us to see Christ modeled and lived out, to see both the life and ministry of Christ incarnated. There is no substitute for the life-on-life, organic development of disciples. We have trusted the machinery of ministry in an effort to mass-produce disciples like Henry Ford did with automobiles. Such machinery violates the natural, organic emergence of the discipleship process - seeing the Person of Christ formed in them. Relationship with those we seek to form in Christ will be required, as Jesus' learning model was relational.

I do, you watch
I do, you help
You do, I help
You do, I watch
You do, someone else watches

This is where the reality of ministry practice engages the Organic Reformation. It is here, in our time focus, and on whom we focus, and what we do with those people when we are with them that is the key to future of the Church in the West. And it is nothing new - it is all stuff Jesus taught us and showed us how to do 2,000 years ago. We have just forgotten. He didn't call us to pastor, or to preach or to lead and administrate a church - He has called us to make disciples who love Him with everything they are, love and serve others, and who in turn, make more disciples for Jesus everywhere, all the time. All of those other elements - pastoring, preaching, etc are part of it as the *means*, and are not the outcome we seek. This "Jesus way" is what will release the revolutionary power of the Kingdom into the lives of people, into families, into neighborhoods, into towns and cities, into nations. This is the hope for the Church in the West. This is the way of the Kingdom.

Reflect

What has God spoken to me through this chapter?

_____

Where am I as a disciple?

_____

Where am I as a disciple-maker?

_____

Evaluate

How does my ministry line up with the rabbinical process of Jesus?

_____

How does my life and ministry line up with the Irreducible Core?

_____

Where do I invest most of my time: the Multitudes, the 72, the 12, the 3?

_____

Adjust

What in my heart and thinking, life, and ministry practice is God challenging through this chapter?

_____

_____

Do

What will I do to embrace the needed changes?

_____

_____

CHAPTER SIX

the **Environment**
of the kingdom

Environment is Everything

As we said earlier in the Manifesto chapter, it is how we live together in Christ and how we relate in His love that defines us a "church." Several passages from Scripture speak to us about this:

A new commandment I give to you, that you love one another: just as I have loved you, you also are to love one another. By this all people will know that you are my disciples, if you have love for one another."
(John 13:34-35)

The hallmark of the Kingdom community is love. The greatest witness of this band of brothers and sisters will be their love for one another. Jesus points this out in another passage as well, speaking of the witness of His body as a whole:

"You are the light of the world. A city set on a hill cannot be hidden. Nor do people light a lamp and put it under a basket, but on a stand, and it gives light to all in the house. In the same way, let your light shine before others, so that they may see your good works and give glory to your Father who is in heaven. (Matthew 5:14-16)

Apparently, the love this community is to manifest is demonstrated most expressively in the acts of compassion, justice and truth done by the individuals and families of the church. This echoes God's expectation in Micah 6:8:

He has told you, O man, what is good;
and what does the Lord require of you
but to do justice, and to love kindness,
and to walk humbly with your God?

The infant church of the first three hundred years took literally the reality of loving one another. Although the early church was not perfect, it did do all it could to minister to the broken, the sick, the helpless, the poor, for in so doing believed they were ministering to Jesus (Matthew 25:31-46). Undoubtedly, it is one of the many reasons why the early church had favor with the community (Acts 2:47; 5:13).

But it is mainly the deeds of a love so noble that lead many to put a brand upon us. See, they say, how they love one another...how they are ready even to die for one another. (Tertullian)

This example of love is wonderfully illustrated during the reign of Julian, the emperor of Rome. Julian the Apostate (nephew of the first Christian emperor, Constantine I) instituted pagan charities in an effort to match the Christians. Julian referred to these Christians as Galileans (a derogatory term). He felt Christianity was a local movement that had spun out of control. In 362 AD, the emperor Julian complained in a letter to the high priest in Galatia that the pagans needed to equal the virtues of Christians. Julian believed the recent Christian growth was caused by their *"moral character, even if pretended,"* and by their *"benevolence toward strangers and care for the graves of the dead."* Julian also wrote, despising the Galileans on one side while applauding them on the other:

"I think that when the poor happened to be neglected and overlooked by the priests, the impious Galileans observed this and devoted themselves to benevolence." And he also wrote, "The impious Galileans support not only their

poor, but ours as well, everyone can see that
our people lack aid from us." (Stark 84)

The Christians were outshining Rome when it came to creating a welfare program that loved and cared for the sick, the poor, and all those less fortunate. Julian was deeply frustrated and his reminder to us that our growth should always come by way of "moral character" and "benevolence." As Jesus so powerfully reminds us,

For I was hungry, and you fed me. I was thirsty, and you gave me a drink.
I was a stranger, and you invited me into your home. I was naked, and you
gave me clothing. I was sick, and you cared for me. I was in prison, and you
visited me'... 'I tell you the truth, when you did it to one of the least of
these my brothers and sisters, you were doing it to me!'
(Matthew 25:35-36; 40 NLT)

How did such a love get transmitted to people through the life and ministry of the early Christians? Outside of the fact that they simply obeyed Jesus and did not count their lives as their own, we see that their lives of loving obedience to the Person of Christ and His commands (the "Irreducible Core") facilitated the environment that allowed for the transmission of loving God, loving others and as you live life, making disciples. It was all about the *spiritual environment*, and so it is today. The presence of God creates an environment in the midst of local church communities, one that fosters and facilitates the development of His life in people. God is love (I John 4:7-8) and life (Acts 17:28). Since He is, then we can only rightly assume that wherever He is, love and life is present. We are called "light" (Matthew 5:14-16) and "salt" (Matthew 5:13), both elements that bring hope, life and the preservation of life. Positively this means we release life, and negatively it means that we slow the decay of death, preserving life. As we said earlier, what the environment of our churches should do is facilitate, enhance, and release the spiritual reality of the new birth in individuals and the culture around us. What that local church should provide environmentally is -

An atmosphere that is most conducive for the creation of life - salvation - coming into God's Kingdom through a loving relationship with Him.

An atmosphere that fosters and allows for the on-going development of life - spiritual growth - as we learn to love God, love ourselves in His love and to love others.

An environment by which life can be multiplied - where the making disciples of disciples happens as a natural outflow of the supernatural life of Christ in the community.

We see this in the snapshot of early Church life in Acts 2:42-47:

And they devoted themselves to the apostles' teaching and fellowship, to the breaking of bread and the prayers. And awe came upon every soul, and many wonders and signs were being done through the apostles. And all who believed were together and had all things in common. And they were selling their possessions and belongings and distributing the proceeds to all, as any had need. And day by day, attending the temple together and breaking bread in their homes, they received their food with glad and generous hearts, praising God and having favor with all the people. And the Lord added to their number day by day those who were being saved.

Verse 47 is an outcome statement of a way of life lived out, of the environment that the Holy Spirit produced amongst them - one of devotion, of love, of awe, of service, miraculous and powerful in the effect it had on their lives and the lives of those who encountered Christ in them and their community. Indeed, Christian Schwarz in his work with the Institute for Natural Church Development focuses on the fact that God has designed the Church to grow all by itself. As the scripture states in Mark 4:26-29,

And he said, "The kingdom of God is as if a man should scatter seed on the ground. He sleeps and rises night and day, and the seed sprouts and grows; he knows not how. The earth produces by itself, first the blade, then

the ear, then the full grain in the ear. But when the grain is ripe, at once he puts in the sickle, because the harvest has come."

The focus here is the "all by itself" aspect, or *automaton* in Greek, where we get our word *automatic.* In Schwarz's view, the role of leadership is to remove the inhibitions to growth. Paul speaks of a divine / human partnership in 1 Corinthians 3:6, where he planted, Apollos watered, but God was the one who gave the growth. From this passage we draw this Kingdom ministry principle:

God reserves things for us to do that He will not do, and reserves for Himself some things we cannot do.

So the task of the human leadership within a local church is to partner with the Father in what He is doing, cultivating environments to facilitate the growth of the seed of the Kingdom. We are cultivators and nurturers in His vineyard. We plant, we water, we remove the rocks, we help shape the environment to the optimal state for the seed to grow and multiply, ultimately bearing fruit to the glory of God. Our role in this incarnational partnership is one of ecclesiastical ecologist - we work to uncover His desired design for a local church community, and then we partner with Him in shaping the environment that will produce it. Again, this is why this reformation must be organic. The ministry of the Kingdom is an organically emergent process, life cultivating a life-giving ecosystem where disciples can be grown for Christ.

Nurturing Kingdom Community

Here again the compartmentalization and mechanization of the modern Western Church is resisting the natural life-flow of the Kingdom. Churches are now processing factories and production plants, attempting to mass produce Christians through their programming. Yet, as we have seen, the work of the Spirit in and through us is more akin to that of a gardener; planting the seed of the Kingdom, watering, it, nurturing the new growth, pruning for greater growth - all with great love and affection. Such organic processes will not be found on the factory floor. So, how do we facilitate such organic community? First we must understand what

Christian community is.

First of all, the Church is meant to be a family with a way of life. Jesus indicated in Matthew 12:46-50 that His family was defined by one thing - *a lovingly obedient relationship with a loving Heavenly Father:*

> *While he was still speaking to the people, behold, his mother and his brothers stood outside, asking to speak to him. But he replied to the man who told him, "Who is my mother, and who are my brothers?" And stretching out his hand toward his disciples, he said, "Here are my mother and my brothers! For whoever does the will of my Father in heaven is my brother and sister and mother."*

We can connect this directly with the Great Commandments of Matthew 22:37-40. This family metaphor Jesus uses speaks of closeness, love and affection - both for God and each other. So first of all, the Church is about loving *relationships* - with God and others.

When we look at the Great Commission of Matthew 28:18-20, with the imperative of making disciples on a global scale (reinforced in Acts 1:8), we see that the Church also has the role of a missional entity. We are to carry the Good News of the Kingdom, the message of this loving Father to His wayward children, everywhere we go, making disciples through every aspect of life. *Life is the curriculum, the entire world is the venue, and everyday life is the methodology.* So this is a major element in the Church's *raison d'être*, or reason for being.

Community then, that shared life in Christ, is a combination of the *relationships* and the *reason*, a *"both/and,"* holistic environment. This is true *koinonia*, participation in or with, the relationship with a reason. Again, the Acts 2 passage cited above is an excellent example of this, portraying these principles in the life of the Church community. The Great Commandments, integrated with the Great Commission into a way of life produces the Great Community.

How then, do we do this? How do we work with the Father to create and facilitate such an environment? Kingdom community emerges from the unimpeded life flow of Christ in His people: His life in us, flowing out of us to others. This is the substance of community. Jesus uses an organic metaphor of *living* water - living water meaning rushing, flowing and not stagnant or putrid, like the Dead Sea:

On the last day of the feast, the great day, Jesus stood up and cried out, "If anyone thirsts, let him come to me and drink. Whoever believes in me, as the Scripture has said, 'Out of his heart will flow rivers of living water.'" Now this he said about the Spirit, whom those who believed in him were to receive, for as yet the Spirit had not been given, because Jesus was not yet glorified. (John 7:37-39)

It was this water in John 7 - the life of the Spirit - that Jesus promised the woman of Samaria at the well of Jacob in John 4. Life in the Spirit produces this life in us, and reproduces this life through us - the continuation of the incarnational work of Christ. When we allow the working of His Spirit in us individually and corporately, the environment is shaped, first in our hearts (Romans 15:17), then in our lives, and ultimately, through our lives: we witness to the transforming power of Jesus.

How do we know what this looks like? This community, organic in its nature, has a number of hallmarks because of His life at work in us and through us:

It is relational - built on the Great Commandments (Matthew 22:37-40).

It is incarnational - built on the pattern of Jesus. Community is modeled, not taught. It is experienced, and not just explained with words (John 14:6).

It is missional - built around the Great Commission - relationship with a reason (Matthew 28:18-20). *It ministers in word, example and power* (Romans 15:18-19). *And because of this:*

It multiplies -more disciples are made and formed into both existing and new church communities, life giving birth to life

It loves - in response to His love (1 John 4:19, John 13:34-35)

It welcomes and accepts - as Christ has accepted us (Romans 15:7)

It gives - as God has so freely given to us (John 3:16; Romans 5:6-8)

It forgives - even as He has forgiven us (Ephesians 4:32)

All of these - and there are many more such elements - are aspects of *being* in Christ which produce more life - all what we call *ministry* - the life of Christ flowing from us to others. The incarnational role of the local church leadership is to embody these elements in their relationships, creating a healthy church environment. Check out the qualifications for Elders in 1 Timothy 3. All of these qualifications but one (the ability to teach) relate to character and home life. If the life of Christ doesn't exist in the home, the pastoral leader won't be able to reproduce that life in the larger context of a local church community. We like to say: *if it doesn't work at home, you don't get to export it.*

So the cultivation of the ecosystem of a local church, and biosphere of the global Church begins in the homes of the leadership. It begins with them, their own discipleship, and their own relationship with the Father. From there it extends to discipleship with their spouse, cultivating a community of trinity: God, man and woman. Then the life of Christ extends naturally to family discipleship and cultivates the spiritual environment within the home. It is then that the living water of the Spirit can flow most fully and freely to other families and individuals, as we continually cultivate His life in us.

It amazes us on a regular basis that the spiritual reality of the Christian life is something that many leaders and pastors need to consult a curriculum for - seeking information on how to lead people on a spiritual pathway. That speaks so profoundly about our training to be program managers and not directors or shepherds of the spiritual life. After all, we know how to execute a business plan, cast vision, foster and encourage volunteers, market our product, etc., but oddly, know less about how to see Christ formed in people (Galatians 4:19). Life in Christ moves us to wholeness and holiness, reflecting the Father's heart in every aspect of our lives.

There is no shortcut for the formation of such community, and the home is the non-negotiable as the starting place. But that is another book entirely!

Communities Connected in the Kingdom

If the local church is then a spiritual ecosystem where living people live in community together, being led by a living Lord, having the same Father, learning to live together in their local cultural environment, then it must be seen as just one part of a larger, interconnected whole - a biosphere (a term coined by geologist Edward Suess in 1875 - *"the place on earth's surface where life dwells"*). A local church functions as a dynamic and complex component (ecosystem), interacting within the larger framework of the universal Church - the spiritual biosphere - making up the One Church that belongs to Christ. The result is a community life that blesses others (Genesis 12:2) and unity around the issues that matter in the environment of the Kingdom of God:

> *Behold, how good and pleasant it is*
> *when brothers dwell in unity!*
> *It is like the precious oil on the head,*
> *running down on the beard,*
> *on the beard of Aaron,*
> *running down on the collar of his robes!*
> *It is like the dew of Hermon,*
> *which falls on the mountains of Zion!*
> *For there the Lord has commanded the blessing,*
> *life forevermore.* (Psalm 133)

The Earth is one biosphere with many ecosystems. The size and scale of an ecosystem can vary widely as it does in the life of the Church. It may be a whole forest as well as a small pond. We even see that different ecosystems are often separated by geographical barriers, like deserts, mountains or oceans, or are isolated otherwise, like lakes or rivers. As these borders are never rigid, ecosystems tend to blend into each other - they are separate and yet connected, a symbiotic whole.

As a result, the whole Earth can be seen as a single biosphere. In the same way, the Church is separate and connected, functioning as One Church (the Ecosystem) and yet many churches (ecosystems). The problem is that our churches in our day and age function more like isolated biospheres rather than as part of the ecological whole. Or maybe worse yet, our churches become enclosed and self-contained biospheres within the greater biosphere, trying to protect and preserve a way of life that is focused more on keeping people in, than it is releasing them to life that is contained in God's biosphere and His Church (the Ecosystem). Such systems are based in fear and lack the love that desires to incarnate and share the amazing grace that saves, sustains and matures us into the sons and daughters He meant us to be. We must not allow our local churches to become isolated from the ecological whole - the spiritual environment called the Body of Christ. There is one Lord, one faith, one baptism, one God and Father of us all, one Kingdom, one Body of Christ, one Church.

The life of Christ within the smaller ecosystems of this larger whole must be vibrant for the whole to be healthy. Can you envision a global Church healthy and multiplying, the mustard seed becoming a tree? To see that happen the church you lead must have that virtue of Jesus flowing from the hem of His garment, the living water of His Spirit flowing in the midst of each individual, their marriage, their families, the congregation as a whole, and out into the world at large. You don't need to change the world, the whole biosphere. But you do need to change your ecosystem, your local church. Tend it, keep it, and nurture it. Plant it, water it and God will give the growth - spiritually and numerically. Move away from the machine of ministry, cultivate instead the life of Christ in your midst, and you will have an Organic Reformation.

Reflect

How are you currently experiencing the community described in this chapter? In your home? In your local church? As part of the global Church biosphere?

_____

Is the life of Christ flowing in the members of your church?

_____

Evaluate

What are you doing to facilitate the life of Christ in people? Is it relational and incarnational, or mechanical and programmatic?

_____

_____

What are you doing that resists the Lord in developing community in your home? In your Church?

_____

_____

Adjust

What do you need to change in your life and ministry practice to facilitate your own discipleship, that of your family and that of your church so that community can emerge?

_____

_____

Do

What are your next three steps: Personally? As a family? As a church?

_____

_____

CHAPTER SEVEN

Fostering an organic reformation

Jesus, the Ultimate Rabbi

As we have noted in previous chapters, we want to start with the person of Jesus, our Ultimate Rabbi. Jesus is not only our Savior but our example. He is "the Way, the Truth and the Life" and as such surely He must have something to say about identifying and making disciples, leadership development, and the organic keys to facilitating a movement that transforms culture, extending His Kingdom reign and rule in our earthly domains.

As we have stated earlier, we want to know what the Rabbi knows, to do what the Rabbi does, in order to be like the Rabbi. This is not a simple exercise in propositional acquisition and information management, but a lifestyle of dependent obedience to the Person of Christ, seeking to have Christ formed in us and in those we shepherd and care for in His Kingdom rule.

This mindset, however, is a complete re-orientation around the profound simplicity of the "IC" - a rediscovery of the ancient truths of Scripture that so aptly apply to every person in every culture in any period of time. This rediscovery requires a change of mind regarding how we think about and do church. The power of societal transformation, and for that matter personal transformation, cannot be found in the forms we practice but in the Person of Christ that our forms attempt to express and reveal. The "wineskin" is necessary, as we have discussed, but is nothing without the "wine" (Jesus).

As the Holy Spirit enlightens us to what is going on in the ecclesiological world, we discover that a worldview transformation is necessary as we learn to align our hearts to the eternal values of the Kingdom of God, values that express themselves more in relationship with God and others than in tactical responsibilities and duties that do more to keep the form intact than the in-forming of our relationship with Christ. Again, we are all for form and structure as long as the "wine" of Jesus is present in our lives and in our community.

As we take a look at the life and ministry of Jesus, we see some simple and profound steps that help us understand how to foster an organic movement. Let's pause and look at a broad overview of Jesus' process of discipleship (adapted from A. B. Bruce, *Training of the Twelve* and Bill Hull, *The Complete Book of Discipleship*).

"Come and see" (John 1:35-1:51)

The organic reality of the Kingdom is seen here as we note that God has prepared the disciples' hearts beforehand to meet Christ. As Jesus introduced Himself to the disciples, their prepared hearts were awakened and their passion ignited to do just what He said: "Come and see." Not only were they willing to follow Christ, but we see Andrew going to get his brother Simon to "come and see" as well. This is a perfect picture of the organic life of the Kingdom as it not only awakens our passion to follow but ignites our hearts (Matthew 5:14-16) to invite people to "come and see" this most amazing Jesus. In this beginning phase, the disciples began to learn that ministry was neither about them nor about simply serving others. It was and still is about a loving relationship with Christ, our Ultimate Rabbi and serving Him. As we serve our Ultimate Rabbi, we learn that He did not come to be served, but to serve (Mark 10:45). And as His disciples, we are called to imitate this pattern. There is a very natural multiplication element in the organic process because love motivates you and makes you aware of the "other."

"Come and follow me" (Matthew 4:19 and Mark 1:16-18)

There is a point in the organic process of tasting and seeing that the Lord is good (Psalm 34:8), and it is here that the invitation to follow is given. When Jesus invites His disciples to follow Him, He is asking for an absolute shift in their lives, so absolute that the disciples leave their professions to follow Jesus and orient their lives around this Rabbi and His yoke (interpretation of the Torah). Jesus did not demean or demand, but invited. This invitation is the first step in restoring the broken image of God (*Imago Dei*) in the disciples, as it is for us. His invitation is an invitation to a relationship and life with Him that involves us in the family business of restoring broken humanity back to the Father.

The invitation was personal - "Come and follow Me" - not a program or a tradition or a new doctrine, but a person. Simplistically, we know that as an individual connects with others, their motivation to serve in the Kingdom of God is enhanced. Logically, we can only assume that as disciples develop a relationship with the Ultimate Rabbi, live their lives in relationship with each other in the Kingdom Community, that the motivation to love and serve our King and His people will only increase. Love always motivates.

This invitation not only fulfills the human longing to belong to something greater than ourselves, but also facilitates the development of our self-image as sons and daughters of God, participating in the family business. The disciples were challenged to stretch their self-image from fisherman and the like, to "world-changing revolutionaries." The invitation of our Ultimate Rabbi allows for the Kingdom's purpose and pleasure to become clear to each disciple as they now live with a Kingdom perspective and vision for the future that so radically impacts their present, it shatters the darkness of our human condition to make way for the Light of the Word to restore and reconcile the world to Himself.

In Jesus' ministry, His focus in this phase is on the 70-120 followers that were with Him. He is forming a spiritual community that is learning to do life and ministry together as they observe their Rabbi in every facet of life.

"Come and be with me" (Mark 3:13-14)

As Jesus moves progressively closer to the cross, He begins to narrow His focus even more from the crowds, to the 120, the 70 and now to the 12 and then the 3. Jesus spends an entire night in prayer to seek the Father's wisdom on who the 12 should be (Mark 3:13-14). Jesus selects the 12 and begins to concentrate more on them and multiplying His heart and life in and through them. The "12" are the foundation stones for the future church and Jesus is prayerfully and carefully laying that foundation in the lives of His disciples - not a building, a tradition or a doctrine per se. As leaders, we are wise to do the same. Jesus allows the 12 to see more of Him and to know more of Him as His love and compassion for the creation is clearly manifest in all of His activities. This love and compassion not only cares for the broken and lost but multiplies itself in the lives of His followers.

Jesus chose His disciples to be in relationship with Him, restoring the broken relationship that humanity has had since the sin of our first parents, Adam and Eve. The formation of the reconciling Kingdom community is now taking shape and the DNA is being set that will allow for a healthy reproduction of Kingdom life and ministry in others.

"Remain in Me" (John 15:5, 7)

Jesus is with His faithful followers and imparting His last words of wisdom and life as He instructs them for the coming of the Holy Spirit that will empower them, guide them, be with them, and facilitate the expansion of the Kingdom through them. The key act that triggers this shift in the disciples' relationship with Jesus is the Cross. His death, burial and resurrection set the stage for His physical departure, allowing for the entrance of the Holy Spirit. As Jesus departs, the disciples are left with the responsibility of reproducing this life in others and carrying on the mission He began. The transformation of the disciples took on a more radical nature when He announced that He would be leaving them (John 16:5-7). Their prepared and called hearts were left in radical tension and anxiety, as they were trying to understand how the future could be anything without their Rabbi.

Jesus then tells His disciples that He is not leaving them alone but giving them the Holy Spirit. What the disciples failed to understand at this point is that the Holy Spirit would ensure the success of the expansion of the Kingdom. This is a pivotal moment in the life of the infant church as its leaders seek to find solid footing on what appears to be a shifting and crumbling foundation.

The disciples come to realize that they have been called, prepared and empowered to live life in the Kingdom and to do the work of the Kingdom. They have been with "The Way, The Truth and The Life" and have witnessed the "how" of the Christian life and ministry as modeled by the Ultimate Rabbi. This departure of Jesus more radically engages the disciples (now apostles) for the future as they now know they are foundation stones that God will build His future church upon (Christ being the cornerstone, Ephesians 2:20).

The Church is "Plan A" of God's strategy and is our best hope of spiritual vitality, life and on-going reproduction of disciples for the Kingdom of God. The Quaker, Elton Trueblood states the largeness of this reality:

> *One of the truly shocking passages of the gospel is that in which Jesus indicates that there is absolutely no substitute for the tiny, loving, caring, reconciling society. If this fails, he suggests, all is failure; there is no other way. He told the little bedraggled fellowship that they were actually the salt of the earth and that if this salt should fail there would be no adequate preservative at all. He was staking all on one throw....One of the most powerful ways of turning people to Christ is by loving others with the great love of God....If there should emerge in our day such a fellowship, wholly without artificiality and free from the dead hand of the past, it would be an exciting event of momentous importance. A society of genuine loving friends, set free from the self-seeking struggle for personal prestige and from all unreality, would be something unutterably priceless and powerful. A wise person would travel any distance to join it. (cited in* The Complete Book of Discipleship *184)*

The Jesus Way of the Jesus Movement

Now that we have taken a 40,000 foot view of the Jesus' process for discipleship, let's lower the altitude and take a more specific look at what Jesus actually did in the formation of His disciples and leaders, and the steps He took to foster a movement.

To begin, let us state an obvious assumption here. Jesus was clearly sent, chosen and prepared by the Father to be the reconciling and restoring agent (propitiation for our sins, Romans 3:23-25) for humanity. As powerful and absolute as this is, Jesus was also the ultimate pattern for life and ministry. As the Ultimate Rabbi, His yoke and His way for life and ministry in the Kingdom of God was intended for all apprentices to imitate - not just the original disciples, but all who seek to be followers/disciples of the King. Having said that, let's now turn to what our Ultimate Rabbi did.

The first thing Jesus did was live a life of faithful observance to the Torah, praying and obeying all that God had commanded for His people. Jesus' first public act of obedience was His baptism (Matthew 3:15). How is your life a pattern for your followers to imitate Christ (I Corinthians 11:1)?

Second, Jesus went out and gathered and recruited His core community of faithful disciples as He prepared for the onset of His ministry. Jesus did not immediately decide to go public and establish a regional or national ministry, but called to Himself those that would one day be the foundation stones for the ekklesia that was forming. These people become the coalition of the willing, the visionary community that drives culture change (the 12).

He prayerfully identified the "foundation stones" or "strategic transformers," the leadership community within His group which is known as the Twelve Apostles. This shows us that Jesus sought to make disciples first, and from those disciples He then prayerfully picked His apostles.

The principle here is that pastors are to first raise up disciples, and from those disciples we prayerfully select our leaders, foundation stones that provide the spiritual foundation for the work God will do in and through us. We also call them "strategic transformers" because they are able to take the vision and carry it out, "transform" it into the cultural context. These are "strategic" individuals because of their God-given calling, gifts and relational networks that will allow for the relational expansion of the faith. Who are your foundation stones? How are you recruiting them?

Third, Jesus cast a vision for the Kingdom. He communicated vision for life in the Kingdom of God. He formed the group He gathered into a community and they lived the way together. He not only called them for a mission, He helped them become a missional community that was loving God, loving each other and making disciples as a way of life.

The problem of the Evangelical church in the West is that we have become so missional that we have forgotten the relationship aspect of Christianity. In other words, we have interpreted the mission as "going and preaching the Gospel" and not the "IC" of loving God, loving others and, as we live life, making disciples. The mission includes the Great Commandments and the Great Co-mission - all three define our mission. As we have talked about, the imperative is not on the going, but on the making of disciples. We applaud all who go, and we believe that we are to go. God's love in our hearts compels us to incarnate the Gospel in as many places as possible. May God continue to raise up faithful harvesters!

All of that to say, our missional problem is that we have married ourselves to the task and inadvertently placed the Person of Jesus in the background, setting us up for mechanistic and manipulative tactics, burnout, an incorrect core matrix for measuring success, competition for the Christian market share, a doctrinal and methodological partnership that purports rightness over righteousness and doctrinal purity over purity of heart.

To avoid such, we, again, look to Jesus, who is the "founder and perfecter of our faith". Jesus is not married to His mission. Rather, He is in a deep and profound relationship to the Father. Jesus frequently says, "My Father" - this is the key and source of His life and ministry. He is not submitted first to a mission, a cause, a methodology, *but to His Father*. It is this *relationship that releases* Him to the mission, the Father's cause and the methodology by which He will do it. If we are in right relationship with God, then the way the Father has made us and gifted us should find full expression in His Kingdom expansion enterprise. It is this relationship that defines who Jesus is, what He will do, and how He will do it.

Living in relationship to the Father, allows us to do only what we see the Father doing. The simple criteria that we have used for determining what the Father is doing is:

It has the heart of the Father.

It is within the framework of the Kingdom of God.

It is within the worldview of Scripture.

Jesus was led by the Spirit. This provides a framework for understanding the Church as being *called, gathered,* and *sent* into the world under the *leading* and *empowering* of the Spirit to *participate* in the Father's *mission.* The larger horizon of discipleship is always the world. How do you cast vision for life and ministry in the Kingdom?

Fourth, He lived the way with them, showing them the Father by incarnating the heart of the Father through word and deed. More simplistically, Jesus' methodology involved His life as His *classroom.* His curriculum was the *daily events* of life. He emphasized the formation of character *as the basis for cultivating capacity* to engage in ministry. His focus was more on *inculcating perspective and attitudes* than in developing methods or skills. His ministry touched the *whole of life.*

For Jesus and the early church, discipleship was a way of life. The Kingdom pathway leads to *a way of life.* This way of life is reflective of the *Father's reconciliation* in our lives and the ministry of reconciliation He has called us to (2 Corinthians 5:18-20). If this is true, then life and ministry are one (or two expressions of one heart), and are lived out in the *flow/power of the Spirit.* This way of life is *founded on a common relationship of love* with the Father and His people. In what ways do you incarnate the heart of the Father through word and deed?

Next, He taught the value of loving relationships with others, and how to have them. He demonstrated the heart of the Father is in loving people, and is not found in religion. Jesus then equipped, empowered and released His disciples to their God-given potential and destinies.

Here are some of the things we have learned from how Jesus worked with His disciples that facilitated His movement: First, He identified the core community of disciples. Then He developed those disciples for God's Kingdom purpose and pleasure. As we work with the Church today, making disciples for Jesus in His movement we have found it helpful to ask three questions so that we could understand how to partner with Him in their development -

Who is this person in Christ?
What has God done and is doing in this person that I can partner with?
What does Christ want to do through this person's life and ministry?

Once you have prayerfully answered these three questions, then using life as the curriculum, *form a pathway* that develops the disciple in the *IC*, helping form the identity, capacity and destiny of each disciple. We want to continue to walk with them in the incarnational and relational pathway of Jesus.

How did Jesus do this? He began to **involve** the disciples in ministry with Him and even sent them out early on in their training process. The formation of spiritual revolutionaries requires that they engage early in the process with specific assignments that form both their character and God-given skill sets for Kingdom expansion.

He **empowered and released** first the Twelve and then the Seventy to do ministry without Him. As the movement began to take shape, Jesus empowered and released the band of disciples to do ministry. This is more than the "under-growth" principle (you can grow as long as you are under me). We believe submission to Christ and the Christ in a leader is absolute. However, the disciple needs to flex their wings and fly - under supervision or in relational "edit-ability." Joseph R. Meyers uses this term "edit-ability" (the editor serves to clarify the voice of the author). As we empower and release disciples to serve alongside us in ministry, we are seeking to sharpen the purity of the Christ that is within them.

Jesus **debriefed** their efforts and clarified their understanding by focusing on fully explaining the Kingdom to His core community. He continued to do public ministry, teaching the crowds in parables. This debrief was critical as it constantly re-oriented the disciples back around the *IC* - the things in life that mattered - as was the case in Luke 10. The disciples return from their mission rather awestruck by their success, "Lord, even the demons are subject to us in your name!" (Luke 10:17). Jesus quickly adjusts this flaw in their character by saying, "Behold, I have given you authority to tread on serpents and scorpions, and over all the power of the enemy, and nothing shall hurt you. Nevertheless, do not rejoice in this, that the spirits are subject to you, but rejoice that your names are written in heaven." (Luke 10:19-20). In essence, He said, "Don't be surprised by the authority, I told you I'd give that to you. Rather, be amazed at the love of my Father for you. Keep your sonship in the forefront and everything else will work out."

Be sure to debrief your disciples and expand the debrief to focus on what matters and help them celebrate their victories, rejoicing in the privilege of being sons and daughters. Be sure to include character formation in your debrief.

Conformed to His Image, Equipped for His Service

Now let's take a look at how we are to equip and enrich our disciples, forming the process that will develop their three key relationships: Relationship with God, relationship with self, and relationship with others. No revolution or movement can effectively begin without personal transformation and specific disciplines employed to ensure the ongoing development of the individual and the cause. The following discussion is not exhaustive but will provide you with some helpful and practical thoughts.

Developing Personal Skill Sets

Here we help the disciple find ways to develop their response to God's amazing love. These skill sets will help the disciple grow in relationship with the Father and to intentionally seek to increase their heart capacity, gifts and talents to reflect the fullness of who Christ is in them. Some examples of these skill sets are listed below.

The first is *daily conversation with God (prayer)* at an appointed time and all throughout the day. Prayer involves submission. Unless *we take time to submit ourselves to God, the act of prayer can be nothing more than an opiate that relieves guilt.* However you pray, whatever form or ritual you seek, make sure it follows the basic framework of the Lord's Prayer:

Acknowledging right relationship and adoration (Matthew 6:9)

Submission to the Kingdom and resolve to see it come (Matthew 6:10)

Admission of need / dependence on the Father and His Kingdom rule (Matthew 6:11)

Repentance, protection and guidance (Matthew 6:12)

Another personal skill set is *time in the Word.* This is a time when the disciple takes in the Word of God reflectively, pondering what the Father is saying specifically and how to respond to it. More simply, it is a time the Word reads the disciple. The normal process we have been taught is to read the Word of God objectively for information, content and principles to live by - all good, but ironically still under the purview and control of the disciple. As we allow the Word to read us, it results in a clash of worldviews, a renewing of the mind, a tearing down of strongholds (ways of thinking influenced by culture) that stand in opposition to life in the Kingdom of God (2 Corinthians 10:3-5) - all leading to transformation.

Two key ways to ensure that the Word of God grows deep into one's heart is through reflection and meditation (Psalm 63:6; 119:11, 15, 27). These twin practices help us secure the truth in our hearts so that the Word of God reads us and brings transformation. Reflection and meditation help us develop a sorely missing component in the church - wisdom. We have knowledge and information but do not always understand how to apply it in our daily lives. This is one of main reasons, we believe, that we constantly seek out more practical ways to engage our ministries, we try to find "bullet point" summaries and books that quickly tell us what to do, and spend less and less time pondering the depths of God's love. Oftentimes we spent more time filling our calendars with activities that give us more knowledge about God and His will without the wisdom to know it and live it.

As a disciple learns to reflect and meditate, he or she discovers the simplicity of grounding themselves in the unfailing and secure presence of the King. From this place of security they can progressively move beyond knowledge to wisdom. They receive a wisdom that enables them to see beyond the everyday challenges of life and into the spiritual reality and life that is available to us all. Here the disciple learns to reflect on the truth of Scripture in the Person of Christ on a daily basis, meditating on what God has said and what He is saying in the present reality, and prayerfully discerning what He wants in response to this.

The disciple begins the day anchoring in the Person of Christ by spending time prayerfully listening to God through dialogue and Scripture reading, reflecting on the things the Spirit is revealing and speaking. The disciple then meditates upon these truths (or truth) throughout the day, applying them and incorporating them into the daily routine. At night, the disciple then reflects in prayerful dialogue with the Father and asks four questions:

In what ways did I love you today, Father?
In what ways did I love others?
Do I love others because of Your love, or do I try to love myself through loving others?
In what ways did I make disciples?

Developing Relational Skill Sets

Here we help the disciple learn how to take the love he has received (I John 4:19) and share it with others. In developing relational skill sets, we are helping the disciple share the life of Christ through their network of relationships, beginning first with those closest to them (Acts 1:8: Jerusalem, Judea, Samaria and beyond). Learning how to navigate the fear-based tapestry of the human heart from the place of a reconciled love allows transformational life-on-life ministry to happen. It's from the place of our reconciliation with the Father through Christ that we are able to minister His life to others. But the reconciliation itself is only the beginning. We must learn to love others with His love where they are currently at in life without expectation of ourselves being loved in return. Navigating such relationships requires skills based in this reconciliation. Teaching our disciples and modeling for them how to love, how to accept, how to forgive and how to resolve conflicts is essential. After all, we are most like God when we are making peace (Matthew 5:9).

What we want is to help the disciple learn how to navigate the relational world. Learning how to deal with internal conflict is a must in properly interpreting the words and actions of others. The next step is to help our disciples learn how to resolve conflict with others. Since reconciliation is the primary ministry of the Church (2 Corinthians 5:18-19), then we need to become quite skilled in conflict resolution.

These relational skill sets are not just designed for ministry advancement but also for *life* - beginning with family. Several relational tools need to be taught to our disciples:

Learning how to speak your heart.
Learning how to hear the heart of another (Proverbs 20:5).
Understanding one's interpretive grid. Is it based in pain, fear, shame or love?
Learning how to resolve conflict.
Learning how to see the other as Christ sees them.

Developing Ministerial Skill Sets

This is where we help the disciple discover their God-given gifts, understand their personal wiring (personality) and talents. There are a myriad of ways one can do this today with the battery of spiritual gifts inventories, DiSC profiles, and so on. Feel free to pick whatever works best for you.

We do recommend that you consider three simple exercises that we have come to love. These exercises take some time but definitely allow for your disciples to be affirmed in their identity and gifts as well as foster a rather deep relational dynamic amongst your leadership community, giving way to the largeness of Christ in your leadership core.

We call the first exercise, "How I See Christ in You." The basis of the exercise is to help the disciple understand who they are in Christ, becoming clearer on where the life and love of Christ is most dominant in their lives. If you do this with your leadership community, be sure to plan several hours depending on the size of your leadership.

The way the exercise works is that you single out one person to receive the affirming words. You then have the rest of the group simply say; "How I see Christ in you is...." They will want to share ways that they have been ministered to by this person and how the life and love of Jesus has impacted them.

The second is the "Composite Jesus" exercise. In this exercise, you will want your leadership community each state the gifts they believe they have and list them on a white board (one leader at a time). Then single out one leader at a time and have the rest of the group affirm their list and/or add to it. When you are done, you will have a larger picture of the Christ that your leadership community represents, helping your group appreciate the diversity of the leaders and their need for each other as they serve in the family business.

We have used this tool for years in our churches. Each time it has helped our leadership teams recognized how uniquely gifted we are for the vision God has set before us, often helping us to realize we have more to give than we knew.

The third is the "Jesus Personality" profile. In this process, each member of the team takes a personality profile of some kind and then lists the various personality types/traits on a white board. This exercise helps your leadership come to appreciate the width and breath that is the personality within your leadership community.

Using all three of these exercises allows your leadership core to see the width and breadth of Christ that is in each leader and the leadership community, helping forge relational ties to Christ and each other - allowing a spirit of humility, trust and appreciation to increase.

Kingdom Benefits of the Jesus Way

What is the effect upon the life of someone who you have developed in this pathway? Well, hopefully, they become more like Christ, living out the IC in everyday life and ministry. But there is more specific quantification of what that looks like in someone's life. Since Jesus' pathway engages them in His mission, they receive the following benefits as a result of being engaged in that mission:

It gives them ecclesiastical identity - they come to clarity regarding why the Church exists in the world.

It gives them missional purpose - they come to clarity on what the Church is to do in the world.

It provides for accountability - because of their participation, they are responsible to God, others and themselves to discern what God is doing and decide how to partner with Him in that.

And since that mission happens in the context of a relational communion, the disciples being developed discover that the pathway:

Fosters communion - they learn how to be in genuine non-hierarchical relationships with others.

Affirms differences - they learn to value differences and diversity in relationships with others (learning to accept the irreducible 'other').

Results in mutuality - they learn to receive the contributions of others while contributing to them from one's own personhood.

Overall, it helps meet the "Big Three" needs many often speak about:

Significance - they learn their identity in Christ as sons/daughters and find how to make their personal contribution to the Kingdom economy.

Transcendence - they are involved with something larger than themselves - the timeless Kingdom - which demands that they not live life for themselves but rather for God and others.

Community - they journey as part of a larger organic whole, having their relational needs meet, while meeting the needs of others.

The God we serve is both a missionary God and a relational God. He has passion for the world, so part of the emphasis is on the mission, task and roles. But He is also a relational God that has passion for a reconciled community - so the emphasis is on the relationship, appreciated differences, and mutuality as well.

So we see the benefit of the organic, natural, life-on-life pathways that Jesus used is that they *give life itself,* because of the content of Christ in it all and His moving through it all. Such things are essential to the Organic Reformation.

Facilitating a Movement

Jesus also set the tone for us on how to bring change to our churches, denominations and organizations. As an insider, Jesus was a faithful and observant Jew that did not come to abolish the Torah but to fulfill it (Matthew 5:17-18). His heart was to help the people return to the simplicity of the Shema (Deuteronomy 6:4-9) and loving relationships with God and others (Matthew 22:37-40). In this way, Jesus was a "Submitted Subversive." He was first, and foremost, submitted to His Father and then to those in authority. Here are some things we have learned from Jesus about facilitating change in any church organization while honoring those in authority over us:

Submitted Subversives are relationally-devoted, reformation-minded and revolution-releasing.

Submitted Subversives are devoted first to Christ and all that He is passionate about. As followers of Christ, we do not want to violate our first relationship.

Submitted Subversives are submitted to the relationships and authority structures that are in place in their tradition, whether that be in the local church setting or the denominational structure or network. Honoring and respecting authority is a must for the Submitted Subversive. Otherwise we are only subversive, which brings havoc and chaos, and does not bring life and restoration to others. If we are only subversive and not submitted, we try to change others with our agenda and self-focused attitude.

Submitted Subversives seek to live in radical obedience which is expressed in love; to the point that they honor God with their lives and honor their leaders and authority figures by fulfilling the requirements asked of them. And so, honor the leaders placed before you and do what they ask of you as long as it does not violate your first relationship. Most of what our leaders ask of us will not violate or challenge our obedience to Christ. If anything, it is simply inconvenient or even unnecessary for ministry fruitfulness. But because they ask it of us, we should, out of honor to Christ and to them, do it.

The so-called "subversive" aspect simply involves doing the works of the Father in such a way, submitted to both God and human authority that, it allows for the work of the Spirit to be fully manifest. This allows for the fruit of the Kingdom to develop so that authority structures, in local church, denominational or network environments, find themselves infected with this new life of the Kingdom that bears much fruit in multiplication and the fruit of the Spirit.

For example, a church planting leader in a local judicatory has a vision to engage the harvest and do incarnational, organic ministry. However, the denomination structure and process prohibits such. The church planter leader would then need to honor the process, while seeking to bring long-term change to his judicatory. As he honors what is requested of him, he would also want to stay faithful to what God is saying to Him without necessarily challenging the system at this time. In this way, the relationships are good and honoring, and the church planter leader is viewed as someone that can be trusted. As the church planting leader begins to venture out with some organic, incarnational processes that are beyond the system the judicatory supports, he finds that in 18-36 months more churches are birthed, more church planters are seeking out the denomination to plant with them, younger church planters are rising up, more people are coming to Christ, more tithe dollars being given to the judicatory and multiplication networks and relationships are forming.

The judicatory will want to embrace these new churches and include them - even if for all the wrong reasons, hopefully not. The leader of the judicatory will, more than likely, want to platform the church planting leader and have him share his story and process. At this point, the message of the revolution gets out to more pastors and leaders and true organizational transformation is now on the way, as life gives way to life.

In this way, the culture is graciously subverted to the way of the Kingdom, allowing for revolution to transpire and Kingdom extension to take place as the culture is reformed back to the "irreducible core" of the Christian faith.

Now, let's pause to talk about how to overcome objections and obstacles that impede the on-going development of organic ministry. If you do begin to reform, you will face these things. In an organic framework, ministry emerges as a supra-natural process fostered by the work of the Holy Spirit in the lives of people. The Body of Christ *self-organizes* around the emerging work of the Spirit. There are several key areas where obstacles or objections may arise as the Kingdom's organic expansion begins to leaven the whole lump (Matthew 13:33):

Thought blockers (2 Corinthians 10:3-5) - inculcated ways of thinking that have become encrustations on the ship of the Kingdom. Such things as a flawed ecclesiology, which is dominated by cultural traditions (even those of earlier reformations), or a non-biblical view of the pastoral task are examples of such things.

Theological blockers (John 5:39-40) - the leaders in Jesus' day didn't have a theology that allowed for their own Messiah! Your movement, too, may have theological, doctrinal or worldview issues which will present a roadblock to an organic movement being formed.

Cultural blockers - church and denominational cultures, perhaps originally birthed in revival or renewal, or even the Protestant Reformation, now often stand in the way of the future thing God wants to do.

Polity blockers - governmental systems that are built around "command and control" versus "empower and release" will inhibit the progression of any organically emerging movements. Often tied closely with both historical cultures and theologies, such structures need to be evaluated for their life-releasing / life-restraining nature. The life-restraining elements must be eliminated. We saw a cartoon once of a church board reading their bylaws, "It says here that the will of God can only be overturned by a two-thirds majority vote of the congregation." Ah, church governance! What a joy.

Systemic blockers - within each group, church, network, or denomination there may be systemic things present that can restrict the life of Christ moving. Likewise, there are things which are absent from the system and may need to be added to facilitate the stewarding of the grace of a sprouting movement.

Well, potential reformer, these are the things that are before you. There is a move of God afoot, and we have given you some practical tips on taking your next steps. You will face obstacles, and even opposition, but so did Jesus, the first spiritual revolutionary of our faith. So press on, and read on, as we are not quite yet done - and God is just beginning again in the Church in the West!

Reflect

What has God spoken to me through this chapter?

_____

_____

How am I doing living out the IC with my family?
With my leadership?

_____

_____

_____

Evaluate

How does my life and ministry allow for reproduction?

_____

_____

How does my life and ministry help people grow in the IC?

_____

_____

Adjust

What in my life and ministry practice is God challenging
through this chapter?

_____

_____

Do

What will I do to embrace the needed changes?

_____

_____

_____

Nurturing
kingdom movements

Working with the Father, Organically

As we have already stated, the Kingdom is designed to organically emerge and grow (Mark 4:26-28) all by itself, and our role is to be facilitators of relational environments in which and through which this can occur. When such environments are naturally, relationally clustered and reproduced, a movement is born. Such movements require leadership facilitation, as without such nurture they will either run their course too quickly and burn out, or become "wild fire" without any lasting fruit. The easy example here is between that of Wesley and Whitfield; one left a lasting legacy of a movement, the other left a wonderful collection of sermons and stories.

Such leadership removes the inhibitions to this emergence through our action in partnership with God. This incarnational partnership (1 Corinthians 3:6-9) is one of *divine initiation* and of *human awareness and response*. Jesus portrayed this aspect of our relationship and mission with the Father in John 5:19:

> *So Jesus said to them, "Truly, truly, I say to you, the Son can do nothing of his own accord, but only what he sees the Father doing. For whatever the Father does, that the Son does likewise.*

Such a movement, when it emerges from a particular local church family, or a family of churches, is usually birthed through this combination of God's activity and an aware human response. There is then a "stewardship of the grace" of God (Ephesians 3:2, 1 Corinthians 3:10), cultivating and nurturing the new disciples, leaders and churches being formed. If left unattended for whatever reason, such moves of God can die out before they have run their natural course, or go wild. No newborn is left on the street by a loving parent - mother or father - nor should we do such with new disciples, new leaders or new churches. No young child is left to raise itself. We must partner with God in seeing such movements grow, thrive, mature and reproduce.

Again, loving God and loving others will produce disciples of Christ, some of which will emerge as leaders, some of which will start new churches, all of which will need loving attention, care and development.

Four Key Elements

Four key elements emerge when we want to respond to what the Father is doing in His harvest field. The first is *seeing the potential harvest.* Jesus makes this amazing statement in John 4:35:

Do you not say, 'There are yet four months, then comes the harvest'? Look, I tell you, lift up your eyes, and see that the fields are white for harvest.

After His dialog with the woman of Samaria at Jacob's Well, Jesus points out the lack of awareness on the part of His disciples concerning what God was doing right in their midst. They had gone off to find some lunch for Jesus (where were they going to get kosher take-out in Samaria?) and while they are gone, Jesus has this discourse. Upon their return they "marvel" at the fact Jesus is breaking cultural rules (talking to a Samaritan, who is also a woman) while they are focused on getting Him to eat, missing the real opportunity right around them. So focused on the socio-political realities (the Samaritan woman) and the cares of the day (lunch and who else may have brought it to them) they miss the ripe harvest field before them - the Samaritan villagers coming out to meet them. They thought they were just passing through this God-forsaken region of apostate half-breeds. But Jesus sees what the Father is up to - He sees the ripe harvest, and then ends up staying two days there.

Is this not so much like the Church in the West? We are so caught up in culture wars, doctrinal debates, our own church sub-culture - so wrapped up in the cares of this life that we miss the harvest right around us. There is a harvest in every land, in every generation, and some of it is ripe right now, right before our eyes. We must become aware of what the Father is doing, so that we may respond. We must see with His eyes. We must be sensitized to the Holy Spirit, in tune with Him and with His working in the lives of individuals, in families, in emerging leaders, in pregnant churches, in villages, in towns and cities just like Sychar. We must walk in His flow, as Jesus did, moved by the gentle breezes of the Holy Spirit, in realization of the harvest that is always before us, always about us.

How do we help the people in our churches see the harvest? Simple things can change their perception very quickly:

Have new converts tell their story in public gatherings;

Find ways to help them engage in care for the poor;

Take them on short-term mission trips overseas that engages them in direct witness and not just work projects;

Share the "sin stats" of the culture, depicting the decline of the society;

Explain the decline of the Western Church and share your church's particular conversion growth rate (ouch).

There are many other things you can do right now, right where you are to help people see the harvest. Pray that the eyes of your heart might be enlightened, that you would see through His eyes. Many movements of God are going to emerge in the Organic Reformation, and those who can see their harvest fields and see the Father's work amongst them will be the ones who prosper, yielding fruit that glorifies the Father.

The second key element is *mobilizing leadership*. Once we see what our Father is doing, and we gain His heart for the harvest, we can move forward to developing leaders with the same eyes and the same heart. *If you don't have a harvest, you don't need to develop leaders.* Simply put, we don't need more people to staff our ineffective 21st century programs. We need workers in the harvest field, relationally and incarnationally with others. Indeed, many "leaders" in the churches are simply mid-level program managers, and not missionally focused at all. Not that they wouldn't want to be - if they knew better, they would most like engage. The strongholds in our minds (2 Corinthians 10:3-5) of our cultural forms resist our engagement in the harvest.

No, what Jesus points out, is that the only limitation on the harvest is *lack of laborers.*

> *When he saw the crowds, he had compassion for them, because they were harassed and helpless, like sheep without a shepherd. Then he said to his disciples, "The harvest is plentiful, but the laborers are few; therefore pray earnestly to the Lord of the harvest to send out laborers into his harvest."* (Matthew 9:36-38)

What we need is not more program managers, but rather we need disciple-making disciples. We need leaders who can engage in personal and corporate witness, and teach and model that for others. We need people who will engage the harvest by sowing the seed of the Gospel in the hearts and lives of people, by planting and watering new churches and living an "as you go" lifestyle of discipleship - all of which is proceeding from a heart so impacted by God's love that it can't help but love others.

Each church must become an orchard of leadership development - disciples reproducing more disciples, leaders reproducing more leaders, and pastors producing more pastors. Our Bible colleges and seminaries don't have the bandwidth and enough throughput to meet the needs of the harvest. It must become normative that leaders for the harvest are grown in the natural environment of a local church, mentored and developed as whole people, and not just discipled to task. Biblical knowledge can be delivered in the local environment very effectively, and theological education can also be acquired "as you go," through online or regional resources. Each church must have a "farm system" similar to that of professional sports teams, producing new "players" for the work of the ministry.

There is a *fundamental shift that must take place in the understanding of the pastoral task* if leadership development in a local environment is to take place. The pastor must take on the role of discipler / equipper / developer, and not just that of preacher and chaplain. Creating environments for this to occur is critical, as has already been discussed. Some potential environments are:

Local Bible Institutes;
Holistic (whole-life) personal discipleship processes: one-on-one, triads, small groups;
Apprenticeship processes for all ministry leaders;
Mentoring of emerging leaders;
Leadership development pathways;
Regular leadership community gatherings for nurture and development;
Developmental pathways and sponsorship for emerging pastoral leaders;
Staff internships.

Without such leadership development, the harvest that is right before us now will be lost, and the Church in the West will continue its steep decline. Those churches involved in the Organic Reformation will be those churches who develop, multiply and deploy leaders from the harvest, for the harvest.

The third element is *resourcing "God outbreaks."* In Acts 8, Samaria has received the word of God, and an apostolic delegation is sent down to check out this outbreak of joy. Peter and John are sent down to these new believers and bring a fuller understanding and experience of God. They confront motives in Simon the Magician, and return by preaching in many Samaritan villages.

Still sequestered in Jerusalem, the Apostles did not see the whole extension to Samaria coming, even though Jesus had told them to go there (Acts 1:8). It takes persecution to propel a faithful deacon down there to get the job done. The big boys back in the Holy City had the presence of mind to send some folks to steward the grace of God at work in Samaria, helping it grow, mature and become full of ripe fruit. They didn't try to stamp out the move of God. Instead they brought down the fire of the Holy Spirit! They didn't try to control it, they empowered it and released it. They didn't try to move it back to Jerusalem where they could keep an eye on it, they let the move of God flourish where they found that God had planted it.

As a matter of fact, what Acts is really saying to us is that the Apostles did not fully comprehend the depth of God's love and heart to reach the whole world. Peter begins his sermon by quoting Joel, that "in the last days it shall be, God declares, that I will pour out my Spirit on all flesh" (Acts 2:17). The vastness of that proclamation was not as clearly understood as the Book of Acts reveals. Acts 8 reveals that persecution took the gospel from Jerusalem and Judea into Samaria. Jerusalem received the news of what took place in Samaria and the church in Jerusalem quickly dispatched the "big gun" apostles, Peter and John, to verify and seal what had transpired. One can't help but see the brilliance of our God in this as He moves the two people groups to reconciliation. Peter and John verifying the spiritual activity authenticates the Samaritan experience and re-establishes them on a level playing field and sets the foundation for reconciliation.

When we take a look at Acts 10 and 11, it becomes obvious that the apostles really had no original intention of including "all flesh" in their evangelistic zeal. Peter has to be told in a dream three times that what God declares clean is clean (Acts 10:15). The arrival of Cornelius's entourage had come to inquire of Peter to come and he did so. What takes place in chapter 11 is shocking.

Peter finds a God-fearer in Cornelius and proceeds to proclaim the good news. As he is preaching, the Spirit of God falls on the Gentiles in the same way it did him and his brothers at Pentecost. Peter is shocked, as his explanation to the apostles reveals, "As I began to speak, the Holy Spirit fell on them just as on us at the beginning...If then God gave the same gift to them as he gave to us when we believed in the Lord Jesus Christ, who was I that I could stand in God's way?" (Acts 11:15,17) The stunned silence and awe of the brothers (Acts 11:18) only heightens the truth that none of them expected this. The mission of our God, motivated by love for His creation, is to pour out His Spirit on all flesh. Apparently, this was something the apostles did not fully comprehend. When we partner with our Father for His purpose and pleasure, the life of radical abundance, love, joy and peace permeates our lives as we move with the Father and do what He is doing, setting the stage for a God-outbreak.

How about you? If you had a "God-outbreak" in one of your small groups, what would you do? Try to control it? How about in your youth group? Try to keep it in check? We very often see these responses from insecure pastors whose fear keeps them from being stewards of God's move of grace in their midst. What would you do if there was a God-outbreak at someone's workplace or at the local coffee shop? Would you try to move the "meeting" into the church building, or would you try to resource whoever was doing it, and fan the flames of revival? What if your youth pastor came to you with a vision for a youth service, or even a new church in the next town? What then? Indeed, what if forty people came to Christ in the next town over - would you form them into a church community right there, or expect them to "make the drive" to where you are?

Yes, as you can see, again these are all issues of *awareness and heart* - both of seeing what the Father is doing, and having a heart for His Kingdom, and not just yours. It begs the classic question:

What is God already at work doing that I can partner with?

Without controlling it, without fearing it, but rather empowering and releasing it. This is the heart of the Organic Reformation.

The fourth element in working with the Father organically is through *intentionally identifying and releasing apostolic mission*. This moves beyond just *responding and nurturing* and into *catalyzing and initiating*. We see this well portrayed in Acts 13:1-4:

Now there were in the church at Antioch prophets and teachers, Barnabas, Simeon who was called Niger, Lucius of Cyrene, Manaen a member of the court of Herod the tetrarch, and Saul. While they were worshiping the Lord and fasting, the Holy Spirit said, "Set apart for me Barnabas and

Saul for the work to which I have called them." Then after fasting and praying they laid their hands on them and sent them off. So, being sent out by the Holy Spirit, they went down to Seleucia, and from there they sailed to Cyprus.

Here we have a leadership community, seeking God together, apparently all "on the same page" in heart and mind. This community is able to hear through the gifting of its members the will of God, and set apart two of their number for intentional mission. We note that this doesn't just seem to be Paul and Barnabas' idea - the leadership community affirms the call, empowers them and releases them under the direction of the Holy Spirit as a singular act of intentionality. The text records that they were sent off by the leadership, and sent out by the Holy Spirit, a wonderful display of the incarnational partnership between God and His community.

What these leaders realized was that *all Christianity is lived out globally*, an intentional "as you go" response to the Great Commission of Matthew 28:18-20 and the directive of Jesus in Acts 1:8. The local church expresses itself in local, regional and global mission by establishing new communities of Christ everywhere He calls them to go - in their city, the next town over, another part of the country or somewhere around the world. The call to be a witness and make disciples culminates in the growth of existing churches and the establishment of new ones. The outcome of health is reproduction, and we are to "be fruitful and multiply," making disciples everywhere we go as a way of life. The call is never to grow churches or plant churches, but to make disciples, which in turn should either become part of an existing church or formed into an entirely new community of faith.

Such an apostolic community as we see here in Antioch is marked by a number of attributes:

It provides resourcing, direction and empowerment like James and John in Samaria;

Clarifies and grants permission like James in the Jerusalem Council;

Intentionally mobilizes through empowering and releasing people to mission like the Antiochan church;

Catalyzes and initiates like Paul;

Facilitates, nurtures and encourages like Barnabas;

Builds transformational relationships around the reason of Kingdom extension as the fabric of the multiplication movement.

Churches that will be used by God in the Organic Reformation will be those who are such nurturing and empowering environments, seeing the multiplication of disciples and churches everywhere they go, all the time. Such should be the goal of every pastor, leadership community, indeed, every Christian, *"praising God and having favor with all the people. And the Lord added to their number day by day those who were being saved."* (Acts 2:47)

The Shape it Takes

There is no predetermined form of what all this will look like within a movement of God - it is *organic*, after all! No predetermined structure - form flows from function, with no predetermined outcomes, other than more disciples being made. No, this will look different everywhere, a richly diverse number of ecosystems within a newly vibrant biosphere of the Western Church. But this will be a reformation, and accordingly, some things will need to change.

The first change that will need to take place is in our "Core Metric," or those things we measure to define success. We are outcome-oriented in the Western Church due to the production influences of our culture. Ahlstrom in his *Religious History of the American People* said that all religion in America was "eminently pragmatic." In other words, we like stuff that "works," even our religion. We want a concrete output, something tangible that we can count and measure. And if we can do it bigger, better, faster and cheaper, then we like that too! (All praise be to Saint Henry of Ford, the Patron Saint of Efficiency and Mass-production!)

The important things are often intangible, hard to quantify, and often found within the hearts and lives of individuals and families. They are embodied in story - incarnated - and are not so easily plotted on a graph or put into a spreadsheet.

We rush to validate our ministries with statistics - the countable "ABC's" - of *attendance, buildings and cash.* Yes, cults have lots of people in their meetings, as do rock stars at their concerts. Many historic church buildings have a handful of people left in them and no transformational impact on the community - this cannot be counted as success, surely. Cash? Come on now, there are billions of poor Christians around the world who are having much greater impact for the Kingdom than that of some of our wealthiest churches.

No, ultimately the only hallmark of success in the Kingdom is *obedience to God.* When we obey Him, we have already succeeded. We leave the outcomes of our service to Him, being satisfied with simply obeying, *"So you also, when you have done all that you were commanded, say, 'We are unworthy servants; we have only done what was our duty."* (Luke 17:10)

Well, what can we measure then? Not much, and nothing should be measured for personal validation. Such validation comes from our sonship, not our activity. Matthew 3:17 shows us that the Father was pleased with Jesus before He entered ministry, because He was His Son, not because of performance. We would do well to remember that. So, what then? Should we not count or measure anything in regards to church life and ministry? How will we know that we are doing what the Father wants, that we are being effective in our ministry? This can be a dangerous slippery slope in and of itself, but we do think you can see progress *through the fruit being borne* through the life and ministry of a church community:

The fruit of repentance - people coming to Christ (Matthew 3:8);

The fruit of spiritual health - people growing in Christ (Matthew 7:17);

The fruit of spiritual reproduction - disciples being made for Christ (Matthew 28:19);

The fruit of love in the community of disciples (John 13:34-35);

The fruit of the Spirit displayed in the members of the community (Galatians 5:22-23);

The fruit of good works (Matthew 5:16);

Much fruit of all kinds (John 15:8).

We look then for the fruit of the life of Christ flowing from the Vine to the branches, indicators of health and vibrancy, growth and maturity, maturation and multiplication. Not the numbers, the human cultural validations, but those things which the Father will call "good." This kind of fruit is the goal of the Organic Reformation.

Milestones in the Kingdom

Those involved in leading or administrating organic Kingdom movements will see a similar difficulty in quantifying progress, especially those in denominations or networks. Please don't default to the "ABCs." Let us suggest some milestones which may indicate progress, although they may be hard to enumerate on the standard forms! Here some possible milestones:

A growing percentage of people in the church engaged in mission through relational and incarnational means of all kinds;

Diversity and creativity within ministry forms;

Life-on-life discipleship happening, especially in the home: individual, couple and family discipleship patterns established;

More and better leaders raised up from the harvest for the harvest;

More and better churches multiplied everywhere and in every culture;

An ever-increasing number of young missional leaders identified, developed and deployed;

A growing number of apostolic teams developed, equipped, resourced and released to start new church communities specifically through witness and discipleship (read: NOT just transfer growth);

An ever-increasing number of healthy churches giving birth to healthy new churches of all kinds, shapes and sizes;

Increased Kingdom impact: more people reached and becoming fully devoted followers of Christ;

Societal change: the Kingdom expressed in cultural transformation of the arts, sciences, business, industry and civic institutions through the changed lives of individuals.

Again, these won't fit nicely on the forms, and will be embodied in the stories of people. Learn to listen for the stories, and you will see the naturally supernatural work of the Father.

The Need for Pathways

As organic movements grow and mature, there is a greater need for stewarding the grace as we have discussed, yet to do so without impeding the work of the Lord through control. Creating shared pathways allows people of like-mind to journey together (Amos 3:3), and become elements of the *way of life* of the movement. They must always be functional and flexible, serving the purpose of facilitating the life of Christ. Such pathways become organic structures that *organize, enhance and facilitate life,* but they cannot produce it. You organize and manage life *once it exists; you can't organize life into existence.* Such pathways and structures must be:

Relational - derived from relationship and engaged in through relationship;

Functional - they must serve the purpose for which they are intended without impeding the life flow of Christ;

Defined - clearly laid out and user-friendly, easily navigable, with expectations and available resources clearly communicated;

Adaptive - able to shift with the changing needs of the life flow of Christ, and the needs of the users.

When many hear "organic" they think "chaos." This could not be further from the truth. God has placed structures in all natural life forms, from DNA to cell walls, from skeletal structure to the respiratory system. Organic life has structures within it. Structures are needed for life to function in a healthy way. What kind of structures they are and how well they serve the purpose of that life is what is important. Many existing structures will be useful in the Organic Reformation, but yet again, some will need to change to allow movements to flourish.

On the strategic level, each organization or denomination must think of three major pathways, all of which we have discussed in our book *A New Testament Trilogy* (110-114). Here we discuss the "Corporate Life-Sphere" of the Church. Relational, functional, defined and adaptive pathways are needed for each of the following:

Leadership emergence - developing new pastoral leaders from the harvest for the harvest;

Church health and fruitfulness - assessments and developmental tools and means to monitor and facilitate health leading to fruitfulness and multiplication;

Church multiplication - define resourcing pathways to assist those people and churches specifically called to multiplication, with an openness and flexibility to allow for, and resource Samaritan outbreaks.

These are three key big-picture pathways that are non-negotiable. Leaders in organic movements have developed or access resourcing for each, with the development of new leaders driving it all. Indeed, the Organic Reformation will be driven by such leadership emergence.

Organizational Culture Change

There is a picture on the wall in the Praxis Training Center, one of a giant blue wave, the kind that surfers love. It has a phrase under it:

If you don't ride the wave of change you will find yourself beneath it.

The impact of the Organic Reformation upon existing organizational ministry structures is one of *change*. They must adapt or they will at first lose their Kingdom usefulness, and ultimately, they will collapse and die. Many are in the throes of this already; dried up, fruitless fig trees, withering to death. This is not a judgmental statement on our part, just an observation, one which can no longer be denied. The Church in the West is in steep, rapid decline. All the statistical indicators point this out, as does the increasing marginal nature of the influence of the Church in the lives of individuals and families, and the culture as a whole.

For this we have placed the blame most often on those outside the churches, deriding the culture as it moves away from its historic association with cultural Christianity. We say *cultural Christianity*, because not all of what has been in and of the Church has any attachment to the Scripture, either in belief or practice, which is what the original Protestant Reformation was all about. Perhaps we have not *reformed*, or returned, far enough. Yes, culture has changed, but that is not really the issue. The real issue is that the current operant forms of "church" and denominational organizations are rooted in *history and ecclesiological tradition*, and not the Scripture. Now, as we have said, we revere the historic Church and all that it has brought us, but much of the uniform expression in the Western Church is rooted either in the era of the Protestant Reformation or in the evangelicalism of the Great Awakenings. The eternal Gospel, vibrant and life changing is locked in 16th to 19th Century forms, stuck both too far away from Scripture and too far away from the culture of our current time. Add to that the consumeristic and business-like approach we have adapted for our new ecclesiology and you have the makings of a well-organized machine with an incredible marketing strategy and product, but lacking the vibrant life of the Kingdom that brings transformation to individuals, families, neighborhoods, cities, etc. We need a current incarnation of the ancient New Testament.

As we said, external culture is not the issue. We don't need to flex to be relevant to the culture. We need to change to become relevant expressions of the New Testament. It is not the external society which needs to change, but the culture within the Church, and that culture is dominated by archaic organizations and inflexible institutions. Organizations and institutions are in and of themselves not bad things (the Organic Reformation itself will spawn many of these things) but it is the archaic and inflexible nature that is of issue. Jesus said that we should not destroy the old wineskins and lose the mature wine, but form new wineskins for the new wine (Luke 5:37-39).

So, this leaves us with choices to make. Within our organizational structures, there are cultural ways of doing things. Where these are merely historical, they are problematic, potentially standing in the way of the organic emergence of the life of Christ in our churches. Where such elements align well with the New Testament, they can be excellent tools for facilitating and nurturing that life. Those who have said that we are in a "post-denominational era" misunderstand this. While many historical movements, denominations and church networks will pass away, new ones of new kinds will simply emerge, along with many of the existing denominational wineskins revitalizing themselves, *shedding the historical in favor of the biblical.* Do you doubt this is possible? We see it even now with several denominations reorienting themselves around core New Testament principles - *with almost immediate effect.* Many more regional judicatories and area church networks are pursuing the same pathway back to the Scripture, going on, as we have said elsewhere in our writings, a journey of radical *re-discovery.* They are simply embracing once again, by God's grace, the truth of the New Testament Scriptures.

The Scriptures, by the way, say almost nothing about form of church. There is no "biblical way" of "doing church" discernable in the New Testament. A lot of principles can be drawn from the ministry of Jesus and His disciples, but very few tangible "church activities" can be found there. They met every day. They met in the Temple, in the Synagogue, in the homes, by the river, on a beach, etc. They have leaders called disciples, elders, deacons, apostles, prophets, evangelists, pastors and teachers whom they appoint or they elect. It seems that what we see here is that Christ appoints leadership in His Church which the other leaders and disciples affirm. The metaphor for leadership we most often see used, by both Jesus in His teachings and the Apostles in their writings, is that of spiritual parent. Jesus speaks to his hearers that way and the Apostles write to individuals and churches using the same metaphor (John 13:33, 1 Corinthians 4:15, 1 John 2:1, Galatians 4:19, Philippians 2:22). So once you figure out what the ultimate "form" of church is, then you can move on to simpler things like unraveling the Gordian Knot, finishing some of Einstein's equations relating to the time-space continuum and bringing peace to the Middle East while decoding the number of the Anti-Christ. All attempts to say we must do church this way are eisegetical in nature, reading into the text our own historical and doctrinal bias.

So where does that leave us? In regards to the work of the ministry, organizations and institutions, they are neither bad nor good. It is the content of such things - their nature - which makes them useful for facilitating the life of Christ in movements, or not. They too, are pathways and structures, and must be *relational, functional, defined* and *adaptive* in nature, all the while have at their core the person of Jesus Christ and the core of His teaching (namely to love God with everything we are, to love others even as we are loved and to have a lifestyle of making disciples all the time, everywhere we go). These elements of the "Irreducible Core" become the evaluative criteria of all life and ministry, and for all organizational systems and structures, at the local, regional, national or international level.

Does what we do facilitate people personally knowing the transforming love of God, loving Him in return?

Does what we do help people obtain a right perspective of themselves through the lens of God's love in such a way that they share that love in and through healthy relationships with others?

Does what we do help people become healthy, mature reproducing disciples of Jesus Christ, and become more devoted to Him, to His people and to His mission of reconciliation?

The more your organizational culture can align with these things, the more effective it will be in Kingdom extension, and the greater potential for surviving the Organic Reformation. The more divergent you are from this Core, the less likely your organization will be around in twenty years in any viable form. Reform! Return to the truth of the New Testament Scriptures! The Organic Reformation is now. The Revolution of the Church unleashed is coming, a spiritual bulldozer you will not be able to stop (may your organization not be in the way - reform now!) The appointed time for this Organic Reformation is at hand. The choice is yours. May you choose to partner with what the Father is doing as He reforms His Church so that you are ready to work with Him in the coming spiritual revolution in the West.

Reflect

What are the three main things God spoke to you through this chapter?

_____

_____

_____

What is the Father doing that you need to partner with?

_____

_____

Evaluate

How well is your incarnational partnership with the Lord doing right now?

_____

_____

Adjust

How does your organization (local church or denomination) align in its structure, culture and ministry practice with the "Irreducible Core?"

_____

_____

_____

Do

What are your next steps in cultivating an organic movement where you live?

_____

_____

_____

Bibliography

Ahlstrom, Sydney E. *A Religious History of the American People.*
New Haven: Yale University Press, 1974.

Barna, George. *The Second Coming of the Church.* Nashville:
Thomas Nelson, 2001.

Chambers, Oswald. *Studies in the Sermon on the Mount.* Grand
Rapids: Discovery House Publishers, 2000.

Friends. Executive Producers David Crane, Marta Kauffman
and Kevin Bright. NBC. 1994-2004.

Heschel, Joshua. *God in Search of Man.* New York: Farrar,
Strauss and Giroux, 1993.

Hull, Bill. *Choose the Life: Exploring a Faith that Embraces
Discipleship.* Grand Rapids: BakerBooks, 2004.

Johnston, Tom, and Mike Perkinson. *A New Testament Trilogy:
Our God, Ourselves and Our Community - A Journey of
Radical Rediscovery.* St. Charles: ChurchSmart
Resources, 2005. *(http://www.praxismedia.org)*

King, Martin Luther, Jr. Martin Luther King Jr. *I Have A Dream:
Writings and Speeches That Changed the World.* Ed.
James M. Washington. New York: HarperOne, 1992.

Kinnaman, David. *unChristian: What a Generation Really Thinks
About Christianity…and Why It Matters.* Ada:
BakerBooks, 2007.

Nolan, Albert. *Jesus Before Christianity.* New York:
Orbis Books, 2001.

Olsen, David T. *American Church in Crisis.* Grand Rapids:
    Zondervan, 2008.

Stark, Rodney. *The Rise of Christianity: A Sociologist Reconsiders
    History.* Princeton: Princeton University Press, 1996.

Tertullian. (2009). *Church Fathers: The Apology (Tertullian).*
    Chapter 39, Retrieved from New Advent website,
    September 30, 2009:
    http://www.newadvent.org/fathers/0301.htm/

The Lord of the Rings: The Fellowship of the Ring. Director Peter
    Jackson. New Line Cinema, 2001.

The Matrix. Directors Andy and Larry Wachowski. Warner
    Brothers, 1999.

Young, Brad H. *Meet the Rabbis: Rabbinic Thought and the Teachings
    of Jesus.* Peabody: Hendrickson Publishers, 2007.